out of mind

I wasted time and now doth time waste me

well as to see

is in   able

Meanw
flying n

Come

Time   roughest day

cures all things

How Many?

How many seconds in a minute?
Sixty, and no more in it.

How many minutes in an hour?
Sixty for sun and shower.

How many hours in a day?
Twenty-four for work and play.

How many days in a week?
Seven both to hear and speak.

How many weeks in a month?
Four, as the swift moon runn'th.

How many months in a year?
Twelve the almanack makes clear.

How many years in an age?
One hundred says the sage.

How many ages in time?
No one knows the rhyme.

Christina Rossetti

THE
OXFORD TREASURY
OF
TIME
POEMS

Oxford University Press, Great Clarendon Street, Oxford OX2 6DP

Oxford New York
Athens Auckland Bangkok Bogota
Buenos Aires Calcutta Chennai Cape Town Dar es Salaam
Delhi Florence Hong Kong Istanbul Karachi
Kuala Lumpur Mumbai Madrid Melbourne
Mexico City Nairobi Paris São Paulo Singapore
Taipei Tokyo Toronto Warsaw

and associated companies in
Berlin Ibadan

Oxford is a trade mark of Oxford University Press

This selection and arrangement © Michael Harrison and Christopher Stuart-Clark 1998
First published 1998
First published by Oxford in the United States 1999

A CIP catalogue record for this book is available from the British Library
Library of Congress Catalog Card Number: 98 - 5382

Cover illustration by Elaine Cox
Typeset by Getset (BTS) Ltd, Eynsham, Oxford

ISBN 0 19 276175 7

Printed in Spain

THE
OXFORD TREASURY
OF
TIME
POEMS

Michael Harrison
and Christopher Stuart-Clark

Oxford University Press
Oxford New York Toronto

CONTENTS

How Many? *Christina Rossetti* 4

Is there such a thing as day?

Will There Really Be a 'Morning'? *Emily Dickinson* 13
Half-Past Two *U. A. Fanthorpe* 14
Lock up Your Clocks *Philip Gross* 16
Potato Clock *Roger McGough* 18
Tick-Tock Talk *David McCord* 19
Small Dawn Song *Philip Gross* 21
April Rise *Laurie Lee* 22
Loveliest of Trees *A. E. Housman* 23
Tomorrow Wonders *Russell Hoban* 24
Doing My Homework *John Corben* 25
The Ostrich Is a Silly Bird *Mary E. Wilkins Freeman* 26
The Once that Never Was *Barbara Giles* 27
Talking Time-Travel Blues *Adrian Rumble* 28
Off to Outer Space Tomorrow Morning *Norman Nicholson* 30

And God stepped out on space

i thank You God *E. E. Cummings* 31
The Creation *James Weldon Johnson* 32
Spell of Creation *Kathleen Raine* 36
Humming-Bird *D. H. Lawrence* 38

Days I have held, days I have lost

Morning *Dionne Brand* 39
Composed upon Westminster Bridge *William Wordsworth* 40
Midsummer, Tobago *Derek Walcott* 41
Sunset *June Crebbin* 42
Quieter than Snow *Berlie Doherty* 43
A Day in Autumn *R. S. Thomas* 44
BC:AD *U. A. Fanthorpe* 45
I Stood on a Tower in the Wet *Alfred, Lord Tennyson* 46
A Prehistoric Camp *Andrew Young* 47

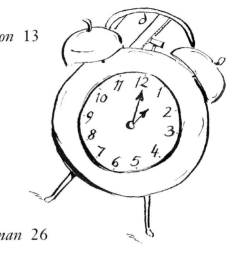

Poem in June   *Milton Acorn*   48
Adlestrop   *Edward Thomas*   49
September   *John Mole*   50

I'll tell you, shall I, something I remember?

On Finding an Old Photograph   *Wendy Cope*   51
Snapshotland   *Sylvia Kantaris*   52
Three or So   *Berlie Doherty*   54
It was Long Ago   *Eleanor Farjeon*   56
Piano   *D. H. Lawrence*   58
Rondeau   *James Leigh Hunt*   59
The Road not Taken   *Robert Frost*   60
Burnt Norton   *T. S. Eliot*   61

The lapse of time and rivers is the same

A Comparison   *William Cowper*   63
The Negro Speaks of Rivers   *Langston Hughes*   64
As I Walked out one Evening   *W. H. Auden*   66
Dover Beach   *Matthew Arnold*   70
Like as the Waves   *William Shakespeare*   72

Time will say nothing but I told you so

Who?   *Charles Causley*   73
If I Could Tell You   *W. H. Auden*   74
Answer July   *Emily Dickinson*   75
Uncle Time   *Dennis Scott*   77
All Hushed and Still   *Emily Brontë*   78
The Night will Never Stay   *Eleanor Farjeon*   79
Parting in Wartime   *Frances Cornford*   80
Egypt's Might is Tumbled Down   *Mary Coleridge*   81
Ozymandias   *Percy Bysshe Shelley*   82
Relic   *Ted Hughes*   83
Spring   *Gerard Manley Hopkins*   84
Song   *John McGrath*   85
The Way through the Woods   *Rudyard Kipling*   86
On the Vanity of Earthly Greatness   *Arthur Guiterman*   88

What are days for?

Days   *Philip Larkin* 89
To Everything There Is a Season   *Ecclesiastes* 90
Leisure   *W. H. Davies* 92
To the Virgins, to Make Much of Time   *Robert Herrick* 93
To His Coy Mistress   *Andrew Marvell* 94
On his Blindness   *John Milton* 96

Now as I was young and easy

Infant Sorrow   *William Blake* 97
Morning Song   *Sylvia Plath* 98
from 'Auguries of Innocence'   *William Blake* 99
Nurse's Song   *William Blake* 100
Nurse's Song   *William Blake* 101
In a dark stone   *Jenny Joseph* 102
The Child at the Window   *Siegfried Sassoon* 104
Childhood   *Frances Cornford* 105
A Birthday Poem   *James Simmons* 106
This is the Day   *June Crebbin* 107
I am ...   *Rosie Martorana* 108
Children's Song   *R. S. Thomas* 109
Late Home   *Brian Lee* 110
Blackberry Picking   *Seamus Heaney* 114
Fern Hill   *Dylan Thomas* 116
I Remember, I Remember   *Thomas Hood* 119

They say eyes clear with age

Names   *Wendy Cope* 121
Long Sight in Age   *Philip Larkin* 122
Old Man Know-All   *Traditional* 123
An Old Man   *R. S. Thomas* 124
The Old Men Admiring Themselves in the Water   *W. B. Yeats* 125
'Body Grows Old, Heart Stays Young'   *Guy Butler* 126
Warning   *Jenny Joseph* 128
A Long Time Ago   *Michael Rosen* 130
Looking Forward   *Sue Cowling* 131
Into My Heart   *A. E. Housman* 132

Our revels now are ended

Song   *Christina Rossetti* 133
The Fly   *William Blake* 134
Epitaph in Lydford Churchyard   *Anon.* 135
Lines said to have been Written on the Eve of his Execution
     Sir Walter Raleigh 136
In a Disused Graveyard   *Robert Frost* 137
Uphill   *Christina Rossetti* 138
Fear No More the Heat o' the Sun   *William Shakespeare* 139
Do Not Go Gentle into that Good Night   *Dylan Thomas* 140
Prospero's Farewell to his Magic   *William Shakespeare* 142

Some say the world will end in fire, some say in ice

Fire and Ice   *Robert Frost* 143
The Judgement Flood   *Anon.* 144
The Four Horsemen   *Revelation* 147
The Last Days   *Micah* 148
And Death Shall Have no Dominion   *Dylan Thomas* 150

Index of Titles and First Lines 152
Index of Authors 154
Index of Artists 155
Acknowledgements 155

A Poem Is   *Jon Stallworthy* 157

*I*S THERE SUCH A THING AS DAY?

Will There Really Be a 'Morning'?

Will there really be a 'Morning'?
Is there such a thing as 'Day'?
Could I see it from the mountains
If I were as tall as they?

Has it feet like Water lilies?
Has it feathers like a Bird?
Is it brought from famous countries
Of which I have never heard?

Oh, some Scholar! Oh, some Sailor!
Oh, some Wise Man from the skies!
Please to tell a little Pilgrim
Where the place called 'Morning' lies!

Emily Dickinson

Half-Past Two

Once upon a schooltime
He did Something Very Wrong
(I forget what it was).

And She said he'd done
Something Very Wrong, and must
Stay in the school-room till half-past two.

(Being cross, she'd forgotten
She hadn't taught him Time.
He was too scared at being wicked to remind her.)

He knew a lot of time: he knew
Gettinguptime, timeyouwereofftime,
Timetogohomenowtime, TVtime,

Timeformykisstime (that was Grantime).
All the important times he knew,
But not half-past two.

He knew the clockface, the little eyes
And two long legs for walking,
But he couldn't click its language,

So he waited, beyond onceupona,
Out of reach of all the timefors,
And knew he'd escaped for ever

Into the smell of old chrysanthemums on Her desk,
Into the silent noise his hangnail made,
Into the air outside the window, into ever.

And then, *My goodness*, she said,
Scuttling in, *I forgot all about you.*
Run along or you'll be late.

So she slotted him back into schooltime,
And he got home in time for teatime,
Nexttime, notimeforthatnowtime,

But he never forgot how once by not knowing time,
He escaped into the lockless land of ever,
Where time hides tick-less waiting to be born.

U. A. Fanthorpe

Lock up Your Clocks

The grandfather clock in the hall
like a perfect butler stands aside
by day. If it speaks, it's only,
tactfully, to fill a silence.
  Until night-time . . .

Then bury your head if you will
in your pillow. You can't help but hear
that weighty footfall through
deserted rooms downstairs. Clocks
  bide their time.

The video recorder flickers green
beneath the TV table. It's alert
as a spider, busy netting dreams
from the airwaves while we're sleeping.
  Lights-out time

and everywhere and nowhere rise
small clockwork cries, squeaky-creaky
like rain-forest frogs or, digital,
the brittle whirr of insect wings.
  Bad time

to be awake. The ticker in your chest
picks up the threat. The night's alive
with tapped-out messages on frequencies
we can't quite catch, or won't, or not
  in time —

like yellow teeth, like claws at work
on the bars of the cage . . . A scratching
at the cell wall . . . Stropping of long knives,
short whispers: *Brothers, soon will come
   the time . . .*

The stroke of one. The town-hall clock.
Far off, another answers, slightly
   out of time.

Philip Gross

Potato Clock

A potato clock, a potato clock
  Has anybody got a potato clock?
A potato clock, a potato clock
  Oh where can I find a potato clock?

I went down to London the other day
Found myself a job with a lot of pay
Carrying bricks on a building site
From early in the morning till late at night

No one here works as hard as me
I never even break for a cup of tea
My only weakness, my only crime
Is that I can never get to work on time

A potato clock, a potato clock
  Has anybody got a potato clock?
A potato clock, a potato clock
  Oh where can I find a potato clock?

I arrived this morning half an hour late
The foreman came up in a terrible state
'You've got a good job, but you'll lose it, cock,
If you don't get up at eight o'clock.'

Up at eight o'clock, up at eight o'clock
  Has anybody got up at eight o'clock?
Up at eight o'clock, up at eight o'clock
  Oh where can I find up at eight o'clock?

Roger McGough

Tick-Tock Talk

Big clocks go *tick*,
Big clocks go *tock*.
The ticking always seems to mock

The tocking. Don't the tocks sound thick
Compared with ticks, whose tongues are quick?

'The clock is *ticking*,' people say.
No clocks are ever *tocking*. They

Make just as many tocks as ticks!
It's sad to see tocks in a fix

Like this: I'd love to know some clocks
That have no ticks at all—just tocks.

One thing you'll notice, though, is when
Clocks strike the hour—five or ten,

Or two or six, say; twelve or three—
They're telling you what they tell me

About the tick-tocks: something's *wrong*,
The sour way that clocks go *Bong!*

David McCord

Small Dawn Song

This is just to say Thank You

to the tick
  of the downstairs clock
    like a blind man's stick
      tap-tip on through the dark

to the lone
  silly blackbird who sang
    before dawn when no one
      should have been listening

to the wheeze
  and chink of the milk float
    like an old nightwatchman clinking keys
    and clearing his throat

    Six o'clock and all's well
    Six o'clock and all's well

The night's been going on
           so long
           so long

This is just to say Thank You.

Philip Gross

April Rise

If ever I saw blessing in the air
I see it now in this still early day
Where lemon-green the vaporous morning drips
Wet sunlight on the powder of my eye.

Blown bubble-film of blue, the sky wraps round
Weeds of warm light whose every root and rod
Splutters with soapy green, and all the world
Sweats with the bead of summer in its bud.

If ever I heard blessing it is there
Where birds in trees that shoals and shadows are
Splash with their hidden wings and drops of sound
Break on my ears their crests of throbbing air.

Pure in the haze the emerald sun dilates,
The lips of sparrows milk the mossy stones,
While white as water by the lake a girl
Swims her green hand among the gathered swans.

Now, as the almond burns its smoking wick,
Dropping small flames to light the candled grass;
Now, as my low blood scales its second chance,
If ever world were blessed, now it is.

Laurie Lee

Loveliest of Trees

Loveliest of trees, the cherry now
Is hung with bloom along the bough,
And stands about the woodland ride
Wearing white for Eastertide.

Now, of my threescore years and ten,
Twenty will not come again,
And take from seventy springs a score,
It only leaves me fifty more.

And since to look at things in bloom
Fifty springs are little room,
About the woodlands I will go
To see the cherry hung with snow.

A. E. Housman

Tomorrow Wonders

'What will they bring me, I wonder?'
says Tomorrow, sleepless in the dark,
thirsting for a glass of water,
feeling his pyjamas rumpled, twisted, and awry.
'What will they bring me?'

'Pennies old and green with mould,
silent whistles, knives with broken blades,'
the clock says, cursing.

'Oh, no,' Tomorrow murmurs,
'they will bring me tasselled trumpets,
kites and oranges, copper horses, sugared owls,
dragons of gingerbread with yellow raisin eyes.'

'Don't,' the clock says, striking
BONG BONG BONG, 'don't,' the clock says,
'count on it.'

Russell Hoban

Doing My Homework

Doing my homework last night
I ran out of time . . .
They don't seem to stock it
At our branch of Tesco.
I asked my mum if she
Could spare me a minute . . .
I said I'd bring it back
As soon as I'd finished.

John Corben

The Ostrich Is a Silly Bird

The ostrich is a silly bird,
  With scarcely any mind.
He often runs so very fast,
  He leaves himself behind,

And when he gets there, has to stand
  And hang about till night,
Without a blessed thing to do
  Until he comes in sight.

Mary E. Wilkins Freeman

The Once that Never Was

The Once that Never Was may be
sooner than dreamed of. Suddenly
we'll find ourselves about to land
on coasts of fabled Samarkand.
There Doctor Who, quite settled down,
will show us all the sights of town
and Lancelot and Guinevere
will take us hunting polar bear.
Luke Skywalker will tell his story
of star wars and galactic glory,
and Eve shall pick us apples which
make people happy, lucky, rich.
There Sleeping Beauty, wide awake,
lives in her castle by the lake.
The towers of Troy, all sunlit, rise
and simple Simon has grown wise.
For everything that ever was
is found in Once that Never Was,
all things pleasant, all things good.

What is that roaring in the wood?

Barbara Giles

Talking Time-Travel Blues

Strap me in your time machine
let the motors whirr
switch controls to speed of light
make my senses blurr.

Batten down the airlocks
make all the hatches fast
blast me through the chronosphere
ferry me through the past.

Take me back three thousand years
roll back the centuries.
I want to see what Earth was like
2000th year AD.

Show me what the world was like
before we burnt the trees
killed off all the animals
and dried up all the seas.

Let me see a clear blue sky
windswept clouds and rain.
I'd love to see the wild Pacific,
hear people laugh again.

I'd like to know how coal was used
and just what oil was for.
Whatever happened to rich gold seams
and other precious ore?

Living in these sterile domes
is simply not for me.
I can't stand food in capsule form.
I need a world that's free.

So strap me to your time machine
let the engine whine
turn the dials to speed of light
I'm Earth bound—just in time.

Adrian Rumble

Off to Outer Space Tomorrow Morning

You can start the Count Down, you can take a last look;
You can pass me my helmet from its plastic hook;
You can cross out my name in the telephone book—
    For I'm off to Outer Space tomorrow morning.

There won't be any calendar, there won't be any clock;
Daylight will be on the switch and winter under lock.
I'll doze when I'm sleepy and wake without a knock—
    For I'm off to Outer Space tomorrow morning.

I'll be writing no letters; I'll be posting no mail.
For with nobody to visit me and not a friend in hail,
In solit'ry confinement as complete as any gaol
    I'll be off to Outer Space tomorrow morning.

When my capsule door is sealed and my space-flight has begun,
With the teacups circling round me like the planets round the sun,
I'll be centre of my gravity, a universe of one,
    Setting off to Outer Space tomorrow morning.

You can watch on television and follow from afar,
Tracking through your telescope my upward shooting star,
But you needn't think I'll give a damn for you or what you are
    When I'm off to Outer Space tomorrow morning.

And when the rockets thrust me on my trans-galactic hop,
With twenty hundred light-years before the first stop,
Then you and every soul on earth can go and blow your top—
For I'm off to Outer Space tomorrow morning.

Norman Nicholson

i thank You God

i thank You God for most this amazing
day for the leaping greenly spirits of trees
and a blue true dream of sky; and for everything
which is natural which is infinite which is yes

(i who have died am alive again today,
and this is the sun's birthday; this is the birth
day of life and of love and wings: and of the gay
great happening illimitably earth)

how should tasting touching hearing seeing
breathing any—lifted from the no
of all nothing—human merely being
doubt unimaginable You?

(now the ears of my ears awake and
now the eyes of my eyes are opened)

E. E. Cummings

The Creation

And God stepped out on space,
And he looked around and said:
I'm lonely—
I'll make me a world.

As far as the eye of God could see
Darkness covered everything,
Blacker than a hundred midnights
Down in a cypress swamp.

Then God smiled,
And the light broke,
And the darkness rolled up on one side,
And the light stood shining on the other,
And God said: That's good!

Then God reached out and took the light in his hands,
And God rolled the light around in his hands
Until he made the sun;
And he set that sun a-blazing in the heavens.
And the light that was left from making the sun
God gathered it up in a shining ball
And flung it against the darkness,
Spangling the night with the moon and stars.
Then down between
The darkness and the light
He hurled the world;
And God said: That's good!

Then God himself stepped down—
And the sun was on his right hand,
And the moon was on his left;
The stars were clustered about his head,
And the earth was under his feet.
And God walked, and where he trod
His footsteps hollowed the valleys out
And bulged the mountains up.

Then he stopped and looked and saw
That the earth was hot and barren.
So God stepped over to the edge of the world
And he spat out the seven seas—
He batted his eyes, and the lightnings flashed—
He clapped his hands, and the thunders rolled—
And the waters above the earth came down,
The cooling waters came down.

Then the green grass sprouted,
And the little red flowers blossomed,
The pine tree pointed his finger to the sky,
And the oak spread out his arms,
The lakes cuddled down in the hollows of the ground,
And the rivers ran down to the sea;
And God smiled again,
And the rainbow appeared
And curled itself around his shoulder.

Then God raised his arm and he waved his hand
Over the sea and over the land,
And he said: Bring forth! Bring forth!
And quicker than God could drop his hand,
Fishes and fowls
And beasts and birds
Swam the rivers and the seas,
Roamed the forests and the woods,
And split the air with their wings.
And God said: That's good!

Then God walked around,
And God looked around
On all that he had made.
He looked at his sun,
And he looked at his moon,
And he looked at his little stars;
He looked on his world
With all its living things,
And God said: I'm lonely still.

Then God sat down—
On the side of a hill where he could think;
By a deep, wide river he sat down;
With his head in his hands,
God thought and thought,
Till he thought, I'll make me a man!
Up from the bed of the river
God scooped the clay;
And by the bank of the river
He kneeled him down;
And there the great God Almighty
Who lit the sun and fixed it in the sky,
Who flung the stars to the most far corner of the night,
Who rounded the earth in the middle of his hand;
This great God,
Like a mammy bending over her baby,
Kneeled down in the dust
Toiling over a lump of clay
Till he shaped it in his own image;
Then into it he blew the breath of life,
And man became a living soul.
Amen. Amen.

James Weldon Johnson

Spell of Creation

Within the flower there lies a seed,
In the seed there springs a tree,
In the tree there spreads a wood.

In the wood there burns a fire,
And in the fire there melts a stone,
Within the stone a ring of iron.

Within the ring there lies an O,
In the O there looks an eye,
In the eye there swims a sea,

And in the sea reflected sky,
And in the sky there shines the sun,
In the sun a bird of gold.

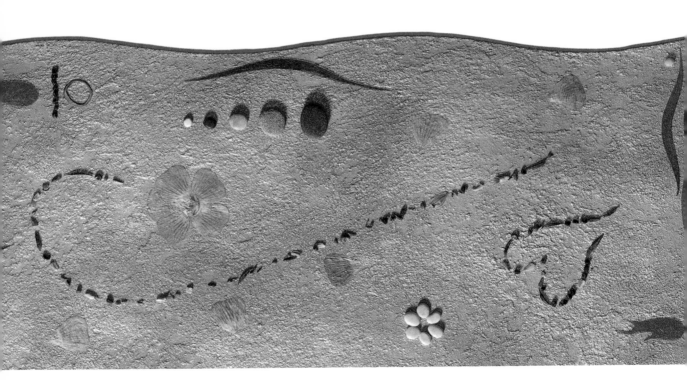

In the bird there beats a heart,
And from the heart there flows a song,
And in the song there sings a word.

In the word there speaks a world,
A word of joy, a world of grief,
From joy and grief there springs my love.

Oh love, my love, there springs a world,
And on the world there shines a sun,
And in the sun there burns a fire.

In the fire consumes my heart,
And in my heart there beats a bird,
And in the bird there wakes an eye,

Within the eye, earth, sea and sky,
Earth, sky and sea within an O,
Lie like the seeds within the flower.

Kathleen Raine

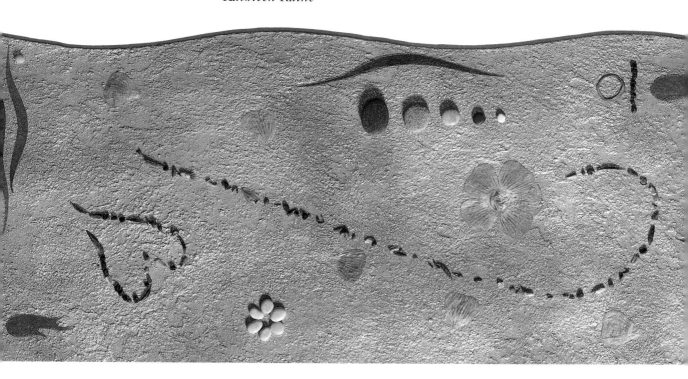

Humming-Bird

I can imagine, in some otherworld
Primeval-dumb, far back
In that most awful stillness, that only gasped and hummed,
Humming-birds raced down the avenues.

Before anything had a soul,
While life was a heave of Matter, half inanimate,
This little bit chipped off in brilliance
And went whizzing through the slow, vast, succulent stems.

I believe there were no flowers, then
In the world where the humming-bird flashed ahead of creation.
I believe he pierced the slow vegetable veins with his long beak.

Probably he was big
As mosses, and little lizards, they say were once big.
Probably he was a jabbing, terrifying monster.

We look at him through the wrong end of the long telescope of Time,
Luckily for us.

D. H. Lawrence

Morning

Day came in
on an old brown bus
with two friends.
She crept down
an empty street
bending over
to sweep the thin dawn away.
With her broom,
she drew red streaks
in the corners
of the dusty sky
and finding a rooster still asleep,
prodded him into song.
A fisherman,
not far from the shore,
lifted his eyes,
saw her coming,
and yawned.
The bus rolled by,
and the two friends caught
a glimpse of blue
as day swung around a corner
to where the sea met a road.
The sky blinked,
woke up,
and might have changed its mind,
but day had come.

Dionne Brand

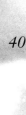

Composed upon Westminster Bridge

Earth has not anything to show more fair:
Dull would he be of soul who could pass by
A sight so touching in its majesty:
This City now doth like a garment wear
The beauty of the morning; silent, bare,
Ships, towers, domes, theatres, and temples lie
Open unto the fields, and to the sky;
All bright and glittering in the smokeless air.
Never did sun more beautifully steep
In his first splendour, valley, rock, or hill;
Ne'er saw I, never felt, a calm so deep!
The river glideth at his own sweet will:
Dear God! the very houses seem asleep;
And all that mighty heart is lying still!

William Wordsworth

Midsummer, Tobago

Broad sun-stoned beaches.

White heat.
A green river.

A bridge,
scorched yellow palms

from the summer-sleeping house
drowsing through August.

Days I have held,
days I have lost,

days that outgrow, like daughters,
my harbouring arms.

Derek Walcott

Sunset

the sun
is having its last fling
of the day
tossing bright streamers
across the sky
ruffling the clouds
into ripples of pink
refusing to go in

until

promising to be back tomorrow
it slips behind the trees
beyond the sea of darkening fields.

June Crebbin

Quieter than Snow

I went to school a day too soon
And couldn't understand
Why silence hung in the yard like sheets
Nothing to flap or spin, no creaks
Or shocks of voices, only air.

And the car-park empty of teachers' cars
Only the first September leaves
Dropping like paper. No racks of bikes
No kicking legs, no fights,
No voices, laughter, anything.

Yet the door was open. My feet
Sucked down the corridor. My reflection
Walked with me past the hall.
My classroom smelt of nothing. And the silence
Rolled like thunder in my ears.

At every desk a still child stared at me
Teachers walked through walls and back again
Cupboard doors swung open, and out crept
More silent children, and still more.

They tiptoed round me
Touched me with ice-cold hands
And opened up their mouths with laughter
That was

Quieter than snow.

Berlie Doherty

A Day in Autumn

It will not always be like this,
The air windless, a few last
Leaves adding their decoration
To the trees' shoulders, braiding the cuffs
Of the boughs with gold; a bird preening
In the lawn's mirror. Having looked up
From the day's chores, pause a minute,
Let the mind take its photograph
Of the bright scene, something to wear
Against the heart in the long cold.

R. S. Thomas

BC:AD

This was the moment when Before
Turned into After, and the future's
Uninvented timekeepers presented arms.

This was the moment when nothing
Happened. Only dull peace
Sprawled boringly over the earth.

This was the moment when even energetic Romans
Could find nothing better to do
Than counting heads in remote provinces.

And this was the moment
When a few farm workers and three
Members of an obscure Persian sect

Walked haphazard by starlight straight
Into the kingdom of heaven.

U. A. Fanthorpe

I Stood on a Tower in the Wet

I stood on a tower in the wet,
And New Year and Old Year met,
And winds were roaring and blowing;
And I said, 'O years, that meet in tears,
Have ye aught that is worth the knowing?
Science enough and exploring,
Wanderers coming and going,
Matter enough for deploring,
But aught that is worth the knowing?'
Seas at my feet were flowing,
Waves on the shingle pouring,
Old Year roaring and blowing,
And New Year blowing and roaring.

Alfred, Lord Tennyson

A Prehistoric Camp

It was the time of year
  Pale lambs leap with thick leggings on
Over small hills that are not there,
  That I climbed Eggardon.

The hedgerows still were bare,
  None ever knew so late a year;
Birds built their nests in the open air,
  Love conquering their fear.

But there on the hill-crest,
  Where only larks or stars look down,
Earthworks exposed a vaster nest,
  Its race of men long flown.

Andrew Young

Poem in June

A breeze wipes creases off my forehead
and my trees lean into summer,
putting on for dresses,
day-weave,
ray-weave, sap's green nakedness.

Hushtime of the singers;
wing-time, worm-time
for the squab with its crooked neck and purse-wide beak.
(On wave-blown alfalfa, a hawk-shadow's coasting.)

As a sail fills and bounds with its business of wind,
my trees lean into summer.

Milton Acorn

Adlestrop

Yes. I remember Adlestrop—
The name, because one afternoon
Of heat the express-train drew up there
Unwontedly. It was late June.

The steam hissed. Some one cleared his throat.
No one left and no one came
On the bare platform. What I saw
Was Adlestrop—only the name

And willows, willow-herb, and grass,
And meadowsweet, and haycocks dry,
No whit less still and lonely fair
Than the high cloudlets in the sky.

And for that minute a blackbird sang
Close by, and round him, mistier,
Farther and farther, all the birds
Of Oxfordshire and Gloucestershire.

Edward Thomas

September

Come back from summer
To your own absence,
The curtains drawn
And nobody at home.

A sudden hesitation
On the doorstep—
Have you been
Too long away?

The lights are out,
The window box is empty,
Neighbours pass
But do not say a word.

Only the hidden key
Is where you left it.
Open up,
Remember who you are.

John Mole

On Finding an Old Photograph

Yalding, 1912. My father

in an apple orchard, sunlight
patching his stylish bags;

three women dressed in soft,
white blouses, skirts that brush the grass;
a child with curly hair.

If they were strangers
it would calm me—half-drugged
by the atmosphere—but it does more—

eases a burden
made of all his sadness
and the things I didn't give him.

There he is, happy, and I am unborn.

Wendy Cope

Snapshotland

In Snapshotland everyone is happy all the time.
It is the promised land where people sit with flasks of tea
on smooth sand by a flat sea and smile and smile and smile.

The sun shines all day long and every day in Kodachrome
or sepia on sandboys and sandgirls who never
stop smiling from the time they first appear, with buckets,
in crisp, gingham pinafores and bonnets on the sea-shore.

Lovers stay in love forever; married couples never
grow tired of each other; everything is always just right.
The dolphins know exactly when to leap into the air
and stay there for the permanent delight of passengers
aboard the pleasure-boat which never passes out of sight.

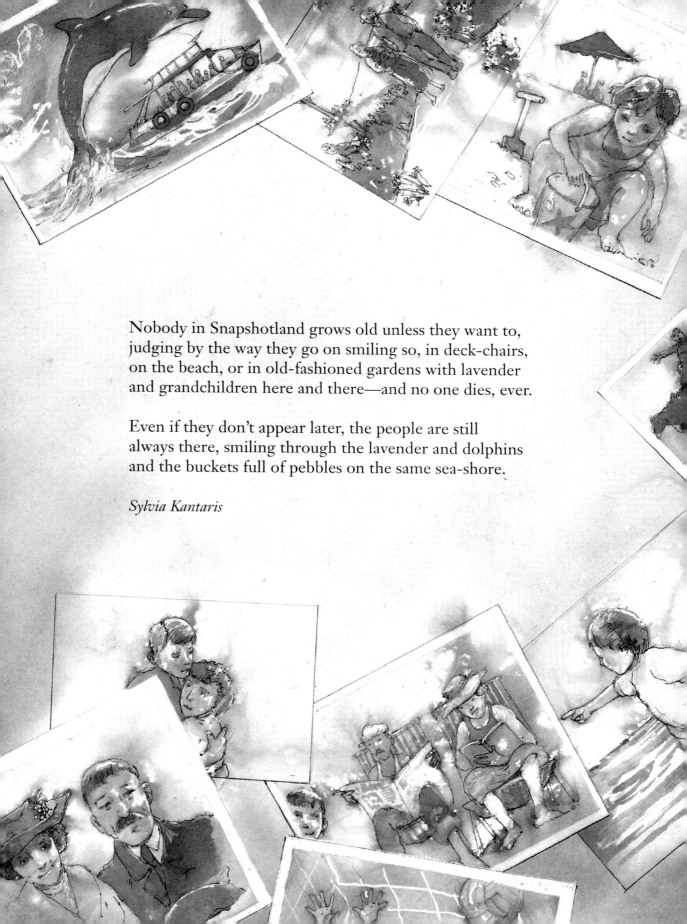

Nobody in Snapshotland grows old unless they want to,
judging by the way they go on smiling so, in deck-chairs,
on the beach, or in old-fashioned gardens with lavender
and grandchildren here and there—and no one dies, ever.

Even if they don't appear later, the people are still
always there, smiling through the lavender and dolphins
and the buckets full of pebbles on the same sea-shore.

Sylvia Kantaris

Three or So

Is that child in the snapshot me?
That little girl in the woollen dress
By a broken door in a tiny yard
She's shy and laughing and ready to run
And shielding her eyes from the morning sun.

I've forgotten the dress, and the colour of it
I've forgotten who took the photograph
I've forgotten the little girl, three or so
She's someone else now, to be wondered at
With my mother's eyes and my own child's hair
And my brother's smile, but the child who's there—
The real soul of her—fled long ago
To the alley-way where she mustn't go
Through the broken door in that tiny yard

Rough men on motorbikes, not to be looked at
Scrawny cats scratching, not to be touched
Down to the railway line, never to go there
Nor up to the road where the traffic rushed
Stay close in the yard with the sun in your eyes
Come and be still for your photograph.

I can hear now the drone of those bikes
And the loud dark voices of the men
And the howl of the tomcats on their prowl
I can hear the scream and shush of the train
And the whooshing of traffic on the road

But the summer buzz in that tiny yard
And the child who laughed with her best dress on
And the voice that told her to stand in the sun
And the click that pressed the shutter down
Have gone
As if they had never been.

Berlie Doherty

It was Long Ago

I'll tell you, shall I, something I remember?
Something that still means a great deal to me.
It was long ago.

A dusty road in summer I remember,
A mountain, and an old house, and a tree
That stood, you know,

Behind the house. An old woman I remember
In a red shawl with a grey cat on her knee
Humming under a tree.

She seemed the oldest thing I can remember,
But then perhaps I was not more than three.
It was long ago.

I dragged on the dusty road, and I remember
How the old woman looked over the fence at me
And seemed to know

How it felt to be three, and called out, I remember
'Do you like bilberries and cream for tea?'
I went under the tree

And while she hummed, and the cat purred, I remember
How she filled a saucer with berries and cream for me
So long ago,

Such berries and such cream as I remember
I never had seen before, and never see
Today, you know.

And that is almost all I can remember,
The house, the mountain, the grey cat on her knee,
Her red shawl, and the tree,

And the taste of the berries, the feel of the sun I remember,
And the smell of everything that used to be
So long ago,

Till the heat on the road outside again I remember,
And how the long dusty road seemed to have for me
No end, you know.

That is the farthest thing I can remember.
It won't mean much to you. It does to me.
Then I grew up, you see.

Eleanor Farjeon

Piano

Softly, in the dusk, a woman is singing to me;
Taking me back down the vista of years, till I see
A child sitting under the piano, in the boom of the tingling strings
And pressing the small, poised feet of a mother who smiles as she sings.

In spite of myself, the insidious mastery of song
Betrays me back, till the heart of me weeps to belong
To the old Sunday evenings at home, with winter outside
And hymns in the cosy parlour, the tinkling piano our guide.

So now it is vain for the singer to burst into clamour
With the great black piano appassionato. The glamour
Of childish days is upon me, my manhood is cast
Down in the flood of remembrance, I weep like a child for the past.

D. H. Lawrence

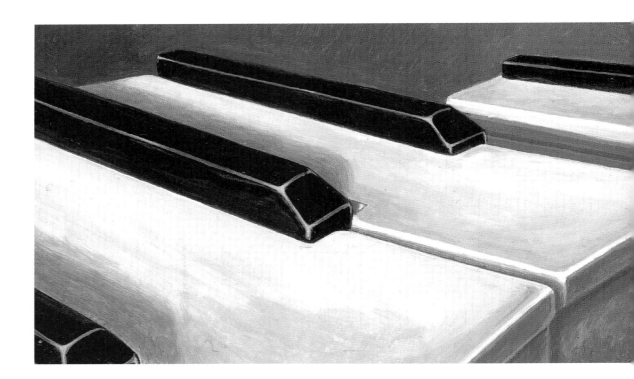

Rondeau

Jenny kissed me when we met,
  Jumping from the chair she sat in;
Time, you thief, who love to get
  Sweets into your list, put that in!
Say I'm weary, say I'm sad,
  Say that health and wealth have missed me,
Say I'm growing old, but add,
  Jenny kissed me.

James Leigh Hunt

The Road not Taken

Two roads diverged in a yellow wood,
And sorry I could not travel both
And be one traveler, long I stood
And looked down one as far as I could
To where it bent in the undergrowth;

Then took the other, as just as fair,
And having perhaps the better claim,
Because it was grassy and wanted wear;
Though as for that, the passing there
Had worn them really about the same,

And both that morning equally lay
In leaves no step had trodden black.
Oh, I kept the first for another day!
Yet knowing how way leads on to way,
I doubted if I should ever come back.

I shall be telling this with a sigh
Somewhere ages and ages hence:
Two roads diverged in a wood, and I—
I took the one less traveled by,
And that has made all the difference.

Robert Frost

Burnt Norton

Time present and time past
Are both perhaps present in time future,
And time future contained in time past.
If all time is eternally present
All time is unredeemable.
What might have been is an abstraction
Remaining a perpetual possibility
Only in a world of speculation.
What might have been and what has been
Point to one end, which is always present.
Footfalls echo in the memory
Down the passage which we did not take
Towards the door we never opened
Into the rose-garden. My words echo
Thus, in your mind.
                              But to what purpose
Disturbing the sun on a bowl of rose-leaves
I do not know.
                       Other echoes
Inhabit the garden. Shall we follow?
Quick, said the bird, find them, find them,
Round the corner. Through the first gate,
Into our first world, shall we follow
The deception of the thrush? Into our first world.

There they were, dignified, invisible,
Moving without pressure, over the dead leaves,
In the autumn heat, through the vibrant air,
And the bird called, in response to
The unheard music hidden in the shrubbery,
And the unseen eyebeam crossed, for the roses
Had the look of flowers that are looked at.
There they were as our guests, accepted and accepting.
So we moved, and they, in a formal pattern,
Along the empty alley, into the box circle,
To look down into the drained pool.
Dry the pool, dry concrete, brown edged,
And the pool was filled with water out of sunlight,
And the lotos rose, quietly, quietly,
The surface glittered out of heart of light,
And they were behind us, reflected in the pool.
Then a cloud passed, and the pool was empty.
Go, said the bird, for the leaves were full of children,
Hidden excitedly, containing laughter.
Go, go, go, said the bird: human kind
Cannot bear very much reality.
Time past and time future
What might have been and what has been
Point to one end, which is always present.

T. S. Eliot

A Comparison

The lapse of time and rivers is the same:
Both speed their journey with a restless stream,
The silent pace with which they steal away
No wealth can bribe, no prayers persuade to stay;
Alike irrevocable both when past,
And a wide ocean swallows both at last.
Though each resemble each in every part,
A difference strikes at length the musing heart:
Streams never flow in vain; where streams abound,
How laughs the land with various plenty crowned!
But time that should enrich the nobler mind,
Neglected, leaves a dreary waste behind.

William Cowper

The Negro Speaks of Rivers

I've known rivers:
I've known rivers ancient as the world and older than the flow
  of human blood in human veins.

My soul has grown deep like the rivers.

I bathed in the Euphrates when dawns were young.
I built my hut near the Congo and it lulled me to sleep.
I looked upon the Nile and raised the pyramids above it.
I heard the singing of the Mississippi when Abe Lincoln went
  down to New Orleans, and I've seen its muddy bosom turn
  all golden in the sunset.

I've known rivers:
Ancient, dusky rivers.

My soul has grown deep like the rivers.

Langston Hughes

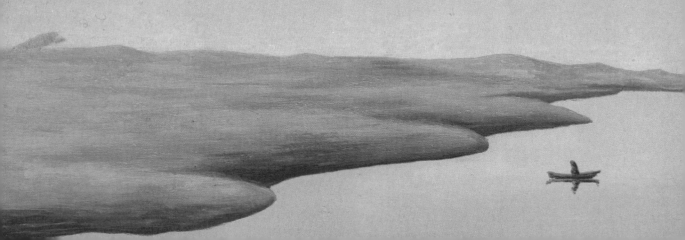

As I Walked out one Evening

As I walked out one evening,
  Walking down Bristol Street,
The crowds upon the pavement
  Were fields of harvest wheat.

And down by the brimming river
  I heard a lover sing
Under an arch of the railway:
  'Love has no ending.

'I'll love you, dear, I'll love you
  Till China and Africa meet,
And the river jumps over the mountain
  And the salmon sing in the street,

'I'll love you till the ocean
  Is folded and hung up to dry
And the seven stars go squawking
  Like geese about the sky.

'The years shall run like rabbits,
  For in my arms I hold
The Flower of the Ages,
  And the first love of the world.'

But all the clocks in the city
  Began to whirr and chime:
'O let not Time deceive you,
  You cannot conquer Time.

'In the burrows of the Nightmare
  Where Justice naked is,
Time watches from the shadow
  And coughs when you would kiss.

'In headaches and in worry
  Vaguely life leaks away,
And Time will have his fancy
  Tomorrow or today.

'Into many a green valley
  Drifts the appalling snow;
Time breaks the threaded dances
  And the diver's brilliant bow.

'O plunge your hands in water,
  Plunge them in up to the wrist;
Stare, stare in the basin
  And wonder what you've missed.

'The glacier knocks in the cupboard,
  The desert sighs in the bed,
And the crack in the tea-cup opens
  A lane to the land of the dead.

'Where the beggars raffle the banknotes
  And the Giant is enchanting to Jack,
And the Lily-white Boy is a Roarer,
  And Jill goes down on her back.

'O look, look in the mirror,
  O look in your distress;
Life remains a blessing
  Although you cannot bless.

'O stand, stand at the window
  As the tears scald and start;
You shall love your crooked neighbour
  With your crooked heart.'

It was late, late in the evening,
  The lovers they were gone;
The clocks had ceased their chiming,
  And the deep river ran on.

W. H. Auden

Dover Beach

The sea is calm tonight.
The tide is full, the moon lies fair
Upon the straits;—on the French coast the light
Gleams and is gone; the cliffs of England stand,
Glimmering and vast, out in the tranquil bay.
Come to the window, sweet is the night-air!
Only, from the long line of spray
Where the sea meets the moon-blanch'd land,
Listen! you hear the grating roar
Of pebbles which the waves draw back, and fling,
At their return, up the high strand,
Begin, and cease, and then again begin,
With tremulous cadence slow, and bring
The eternal note of sadness in.

Sophocles long ago
Heard it on the Aegean, and it brought
Into his mind the turbid ebb and flow
Of human misery; we
Find also in the sound a thought,
Hearing it by this distant northern sea.

The Sea of Faith
Was once, too, at the full, and round earth's shore
Lay like the folds of a bright girdle furl'd.
But now I only hear
Its melancholy, long, withdrawing roar,
Retreating, to the breath
Of the night-wind, down the vast edges drear
And naked shingles of the world.

Ah, love, let us be true
To one another! for the world, which seems
To lie before us like a land of dreams,
So various, so beautiful, so new,
Hath really neither joy, nor love, nor light,
Nor certitude, nor peace, nor help for pain;
And we are here as on a darkling plain
Swept with confused alarms of struggle and flight,
Where ignorant armies clash by night.

Matthew Arnold

Like as the Waves

Like as the waves make towards the pebbled shore,
  So do our minutes hasten to their end;
Each changing place with that which goes before,
  In sequent toil all forwards do contend.
Nativity, once in the main of light,
  Crawls to maturity, wherewith being crowned,
Crooked eclipses 'gainst his glory fight,
  And Time that gave doth now his gift confound.
Time doth transfix the flourish set on youth
  And delves the parallels in beauty's brow,
Feeds on the rarities of nature's truth,
  And nothing stands but for his scythe to mow.
    And yet to times in hope my verse shall stand,
    Praising thy worth, despite his cruel hand.

William Shakespeare

Who?

Who is that child I see wandering, wandering
Down by the side of the quivering stream?
Why does he seem not to hear, though I call to him?
Where does he come from, and what is his name?

Why do I see him at sunrise and sunset
Taking, in old-fashioned clothes, the same track?
Why, when he walks, does he cast not a shadow
Though the sun rises and falls at his back?

Why does the dust lie so thick on the hedgerow
By the great field where a horse pulls the plough?
Why do I see only meadows, where houses
Stand in a line by the riverside now?

Why does he move like a wraith by the water,
Soft as the thistledown on the breeze blown?
When I draw near him so that I may hear him,
Why does he say that his name is my own?

Charles Causley

If I Could Tell You

Time will say nothing but I told you so,
Time only knows the price we have to pay;
If I could tell you I would let you know.

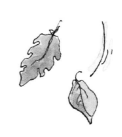

If we should weep when clowns put on their show,
If we should stumble when musicians play,
Time will say nothing but I told you so.

There are no fortunes to be told, although,
Because I love you more than I can say,
If I could tell you I would let you know.

The winds must come from somewhere when they blow,
There must be reasons why the leaves decay;
Time will say nothing but I told you so.

Perhaps the roses really want to grow,
The vision seriously intends to stay;
If I could tell you I would let you know.

Suppose the lions all get up and go,
And all the brooks and soldiers run away;
Will Time say nothing but I told you so?
If I could tell you I would let you know.

W. H. Auden

Answer July

Answer July—
Where is the Bee—
Where is the Blush—
Where is the Hay?

Ah, said July—
Where is the Seed—
Where is the Bud—
Where is the May—
Answer Thee—Me—

Nay—said the May—
Show me the Snow—
Show me the Bells—
Show me the Jay!

Quibbled the Jay—
Where be the Maize—
Where be the Haze—
Where be the Bur?
Here—said the Year—

Emily Dickinson

Uncle Time

Uncle Time is a ole, ole man . . .
All year long 'im wash 'im foot in de sea,
long, lazy years on de wet san'
an' shake de coconut tree dem
quiet-like wid 'im sea-win' laughter,
scraping away de lan' . . .
Uncle Time is a spider-man, cunnin' an' cool,
him tell yu: watch de hill an' yu se mi.
Huhn! Fe yu yi no quick enough fe si
how 'im move like mongoose; man, you tink 'im fool?

Me Uncle Time smile black as sorrow;
'im voice is sof' as bamboo leaf
but Lawd, me Uncle cruel.
When 'im play in de street
wid yu woman—watch 'im! By tomorrow
she dry as cane-fire, bitter as cassava;
an' when 'im teach yu son, long after
yu walk wid stranger, an' yu bread is grief.
Watch how 'im spin web roun' yu house, an' creep
inside; an' when 'im touch yu, weep . . .

Dennis Scott

All Hushed and Still

All hushed and still within the house;
Without—all wind and driving rain;
But something whispers to my mind,
Through rain and through the wailing wind,
  Never again.
Never again? Why not again?
Memory has power as real as thine.

Emily Brontë

The Night will Never Stay

The night will never stay,
The night will still go by,
Though with a million stars
You pin it to the sky;
Though you bind it with the blowing wind
And buckle it with the moon,
The night will slip away
Like sorrow or a tune.

Eleanor Farjeon

Parting in Wartime

How long ago Hector took off his plume,
Not wanting that his little son should cry,
Then kissed his sad Andromache goodbye—
And now we three in Euston waiting-room.

Frances Cornford

Egypt's Might is Tumbled Down

Egypt's might is tumbled down
  Down a-down the deeps of thought;
Greece is fallen and Troy town,
Glorious Rome hath lost her crown,
    Venice' pride is nought.

But the dreams their children dreamed
  Fleeting, unsubstantial, vain,
Shadowy as the shadows seemed,
Airy nothing, as they deemed,
    These remain.

Mary Coleridge

Ozymandias

I met a traveller from an antique land
Who said: Two vast and trunkless legs of stone
Stand in the desert. . . . Near them, on the sand,
Half sunk, a shattered visage lies, whose frown,
And wrinkled lip, and sneer of cold command,
Tell that its sculptor well those passions read
Which yet survive, stamped on these lifeless things,
The hand that mocked them, and the heart that fed:
And on the pedestal these words appear:
'My name is Ozymandias, king of kings:
Look on my works, ye Mighty, and despair!'
Nothing beside remains. Round the decay
Of that colossal wreck, boundless and bare
The lone and level sands stretch far away.

Percy Bysshe Shelley

Relic

I found this jawbone at the sea's edge:
There, crabs, dogfish, broken by the breakers or tossed
To flap for half an hour and turn to a crust
Continue the beginning. The deeps are cold:
In that darkness camaraderie does not hold:
Nothing touches but, clutching, devours. And the jaws,
Before they are satisfied or their stretched purpose
Slacken, go down jaws; go gnawn bare. Jaws
Eat and are finished and the jawbone comes to the beach:
This is the sea's achievement; with shells,
Vertebrae, claws, carapaces, skulls.

Time in the sea eats its tail, thrives, casts these
Indigestibles, the spars of purposes
That failed far from the surface. None grow rich
In the sea. This curved jawbone did not laugh
But gripped, gripped and is now a cenotaph.

Ted Hughes

Spring

Nothing is so beautiful as Spring—
  When weeds, in wheels, shoot long and lovely and lush;
  Thrush's eggs look little low heavens, and thrush
Through the echoing timber does so rinse and wring
The ear, it strikes like lightnings to hear him sing;
  The glassy peartree leaves and blooms, they brush
  The descending blue; that blue is all in a rush
With richness; the racing lambs too have fair their fling.

What is all this juice and all this joy?
  A strain of the earth's sweet being in the beginning
In Eden garden.—Have, get, before it cloy,
  Before it cloud, Christ, lord, and sour with sinning,
Innocent mind and Mayday in girl and boy,
  Most, O maid's child, thy choice and worthy the winning.

Gerard Manley Hopkins

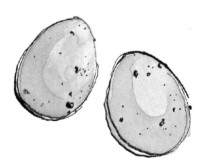

Song

And when our streets are green again
When metalled roads are green
And girls walk barefoot through the weeds
Of Regent Street, Saint Martin's Lane

And children hide in factories
Where burdock blooms and vetch and rust,
And elms and oaks and chestnut trees
Are tall again and hope is lost

When up the Strand the foxes glide
And hedgehogs sniff and wildcats yell
And golden orioles come back
To flash through Barnes and Clerkenwell

When governments and industries
Lie choked by weeds in fertile rain
For sure the few who stay alive
Will laugh and grow to love again

John McGrath

The Way through the Woods

They shut the road through the woods
Seventy years ago.
Weather and rain have undone it again,
And now you would never know
There was once a road through the woods
Before they planted the trees.
It is underneath the coppice and heath,
And the thin anemones.
Only the keeper sees
That, where the ring-dove broods,
And the badgers roll at ease,
There was once a road through the woods.

Yet, if you enter the woods
Of a summer evening late,
When the night-air cools on the trout-ringed pools
Where the otter whistles his mate,
(They fear not men in the woods,
Because they see so few.)
You will hear the beat of a horse's feet,
And the swish of a skirt in the dew,
Steadily cantering through
The misty solitudes,
As though they perfectly knew
The old lost road through the woods . . .
But there is no road through the woods.

Rudyard Kipling

On the Vanity of Earthly Greatness

The tusks that clashed in mighty brawls
Of mastodons, are billiard balls.

The sword of Charlemagne the Just
Is ferric oxide, known as rust.

The grizzly bear whose potent hug
Was feared by all, is now a rug.

Great Caesar's bust is on the shelf,
And I don't feel so well myself.

Arthur Guiterman

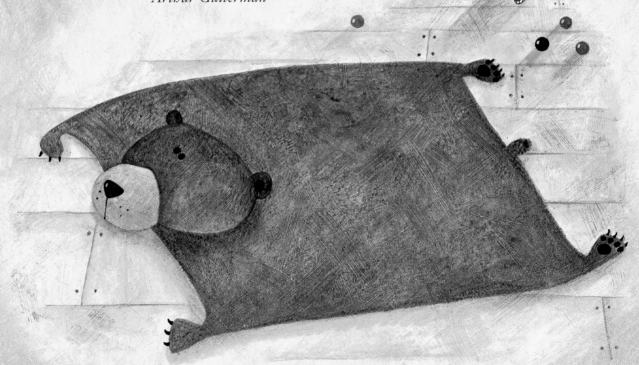

Days

What are days for?
Days are where we live.
They come, they wake us
Time and time over.
They are to be happy in:
Where can we live but days?

Ah, solving that question
Brings the priest and the doctor
In their long coats
Running over the fields.

Philip Larkin

To Everything There Is a Season

To everything there is a season
and a time to every purpose under the heaven:

A time to be born, and a time to die;
a time to plant and a time to pluck up that which is planted;

A time to kill, and a time to heal;
a time to break down, and a time to build up;

A time to weep, and a time to laugh;
a time to mourn, and a time to dance;

A time to cast away stones, and a time to gather stones together;
a time to embrace, and a time to refrain from embracing;

A time to get, and a time to lose;
a time to keep, and a time to cast away;

A time to rend, and a time to sew;
a time to keep silence, and a time to speak;

A time to love, and a time to hate;
a time of war, and a time of peace.

Ecclesiastes 3: 1–8
The Bible: King James Version

Leisure

What is this life if, full of care,
We have no time to stand and stare?

No time to stand beneath the boughs
And stare as long as sheep or cows.

No time to see, when woods we pass,
Where squirrels hide their nuts in grass.

No time to see, in broad daylight,
Streams full of stars, like skies at night.

No time to turn at Beauty's glance,
And watch her feet, how they can dance.

No time to wait till her mouth can
Enrich that smile her eyes began.

A poor life this if, full of care,
We have no time to stand and stare.

W. H. Davies

To the Virgins, to Make Much of Time

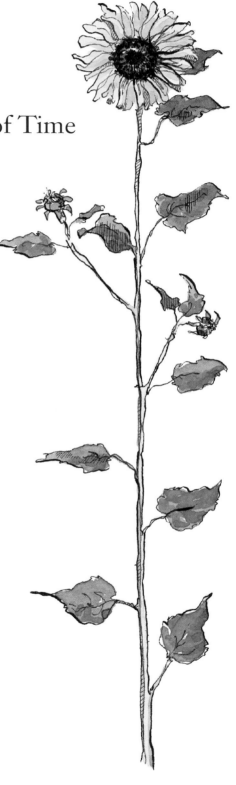

Gather ye rosebuds while ye may,
  Old Time is still a-flying:
And this same flower that smiles today
  Tomorrow will be dying.

The glorious lamp of heaven, the sun,
  The higher he's a-getting,
The sooner will his race be run,
  And nearer he's to setting.

That age is best which is the first,
  When youth and blood are warmer;
But being spent, the worse, and worst
  Times still succeed the former.

Then be not coy, but use your time,
  And while ye may, go marry:
For having lost but once your prime,
  You may for ever tarry.

Robert Herrick

To His Coy Mistress

Had we but world enough, and time,
This coyness, Lady, were no crime.
We would sit down and think which way
To walk and pass our long love's day.
Thou by the Indian Ganges' side
Shouldst rubies find: I by the tide
Of Humber would complain. I would
Love you ten years before the Flood,
And you should, if you please, refuse
Till the conversion of the Jews.
My vegetable love should grow
Vaster than empires, and more slow;
An hundred years should go to praise
Thine eyes and on thy forehead gaze;
Two hundred to adore each breast;
But thirty thousand to the rest;
An age at least to every part,
And the last age should show your heart;
For, Lady, you deserve this state,
Nor would I love at lower rate.
  But at my back I always hear
Time's wingèd chariot hurrying near;
And yonder all before us lie
Deserts of vast eternity.
Thy beauty shall no more be found,
Nor, in thy marble vault, shall sound
My echoing song: then worms shall try
That long preserved virginity,
And your quaint honour turn to dust,
And into ashes all my lust:
The grave's a fine and private place,
But none, I think, do there embrace.

Now therefore, while the youthful hue
Sits on thy skin like morning dew,
And while thy willing soul transpires
At every pore with instant fires,
Now let us sport us while we may,
And now, like amorous birds of prey,
Rather at once our time devour
Than languish in his slow-chapt power.
Let us roll all our strength and all
Our sweetness up into one ball,
And tear our pleasures with rough strife
Thorough the iron gates of life:
Thus, though we cannot make our sun
Stand still, yet we will make him run.

Andrew Marvell

On his Blindness

When I consider how my light is spent
Ere half my days, in this dark world and wide,
　And that one talent which is death to hide,
Lodged with me useless, though my soul more bent
To serve therewith my Maker, and present
　My true account, lest he, returning, chide;
　'Doth God exact day-labour, light denied?'
I fondly ask: but Patience, to prevent
　That murmur, soon replies, 'God doth not need
Either man's work, or his own gifts; who best
　Bear his mild yoke, they serve him best; his state
　Is kingly: thousands at his bidding speed,
And post o'er land and ocean without rest;
　They also serve who only stand and wait.'

John Milton

Infant Sorrow

My mother groan'd, my father wept,
Into the dangerous world I leapt;
Helpless, naked, piping loud,
Like a fiend hid in a cloud.

Struggling in my father's hands,
Striving against my swaddling-bands,
Bound and weary, I thought best
To sulk upon my mother's breast.

William Blake

Morning Song

Love set you going like a fat gold watch.
The midwife slapped your footsoles, and your bald cry
Took its place among the elements.

Our voices echo, magnifying your arrival. New statue.
In a drafty museum, your nakedness
Shadows our safety. We stand round blankly as walls.

I'm no more your mother
Than the cloud that distils a mirror to reflect its own slow
Effacement at the wind's hand.

All night your moth-breath
Flickers among the flat pink roses. I wake to listen:
A far sea moves in my ear.

One cry, and I stumble from bed, cow-heavy and floral
In my Victorian nightgown.
Your mouth opens clean as a cat's. The window square

Whitens and swallows its dull stars. And now you try
Your handful of notes;
The clear vowels rise like balloons.

Sylvia Plath

from 'Auguries of Innocence'

Every night and every morn
Some to misery are born;
Every morn and every night
Some are born to sweet delight;
Some are born to sweet delight,
Some are born to endless night.
Joy and woe are woven fine,
A clothing for the soul divine;
Under every grief and pine
Runs a joy with silken twine.
It is right it should be so;
Man was made for joy and woe;
And when this we rightly know,
Safely through the world we go.

William Blake

Nurse's Song

When the voices of children are heard on the green,
And laughing is heard on the hill,
My heart is at rest within my breast,
And everything else is still.

'Then come home, my children, the sun is gone down,
And the dews of night arise;
Come, come, leave off play, and let us away
Till the morning appears in the skies.'

'No, no, let us play, for it is yet day,
And we cannot go to sleep;
Besides, in the sky the little birds fly,
And the hills are all cover'd with sheep.'

'Well, well, go and play till the light fades away,
And then go home to bed.'
The little ones leapèd and shoutèd and laugh'd
And all the hills echoèd.

William Blake

Nurse's Song

When the voices of children are heard on the green
And whisp'rings are in the dale,
The days of my youth rise fresh in my mind,
My face turns green and pale.

Then come home, my children, the sun is gone down,
And the dews of night arise;
Your spring and your day are wasted in play,
And your winter and night in disguise.

William Blake

In a dark stone

'About 7000 years ago
There was a little girl
Who looked in a mirror
And thought herself pretty.'

'I don't believe you. All that time ago
If there was a little girl she'd be wild
Wearing skins, and living in damp woods.'

'But 7000 years ago
When England was a swamp with no one in it,
Long before the Romans,
In other lands by rivers and in plains
People made necklaces and learnt to write
And wrote down their accounts, and made fine pots,
Maps of the stars to sail by, and built cities;
And that is where they found this mirror
Where once the Hittite people roamed and ruled.'

'So you were there, were you, all that time ago
And living far from home, in ancient Turkey?'

'No, but I saw this mirror. Here in England.
It was the smallest thing in a large hall
Of great bronze cauldrons, statues, slabs of stone.
You mustn't think that it was made of glass
Common, like our mirrors.
                                        It was
A little lump of stone, shining; black; deep;
Hard like a thick black diamond, but better: obsidian.
It would have fitted in the palm of your hand.
One side was shaped and polished, the back rough.
Small though it was I crossed the room to see it.

I wanted to look in it, to see if it worked
Really, as a mirror, but I waited.'

'Why did you wait till nobody was round you?
You weren't trying to steal it were you?'
       'No. I was scared.

I waited and came slowly to it sideways.
I put my hand in front. It worked as a mirror.

And then I looked into that polished stone.
I thought the shadow of the shape I looked at
Was looking out at me. My face went into
That dark deep stone and joined the other face
The pretty one that used to search her mirror
When she was alive thousands of years ago.

I don't think she'd have come if there'd been a crowd.
They were all looking at the gold and brass.'

'I wish I could see it. Would she come for me?'

'I think the mirror's back in Turkey now.'

'I'd travel miles and miles if I could see it.'

'Well, nearer home, there were flint mines in Norfolk
And just where the land slopes a bit above some trees
On the Suffolk-Norfolk border, there's a track
And once I saw . . . But that's another story.'

Jenny Joseph

The Child at the Window

Remember this, when childhood's far away;
The sunlight of a showery first spring day;
You from your house-top window laughing down,
And I, returned with whip-cracks from a ride,
On the great lawn below you, playing the clown.
Time blots our gladness out. Let this with love abide . . .

The brave March day; and you, not four years old,
Up in your nursery world—all heaven for me.
Remember this—the happiness I hold—
In far off springs I shall not live to see;
The world one map of wastening war unrolled,
And you, unconscious of it, setting my spirit free.

For you must learn, beyond bewildering years,
How little things beloved and held are best.
The windows of the world are blurred with tears,
And troubles come like cloud-banks from the west.
Remember this, some afternoon in spring,
When your own child looks down and makes your sad heart sing.

Siegfried Sassoon

Childhood

I used to think that grown-up people chose
To have stiff backs and wrinkles round their nose,
And veins like small fat snakes on either hand,
On purpose to be grand.
Till through the banisters I watched one day
My great-aunt Etty's friend who was going away,
And how her onyx beads had come unstrung.
I saw her grope to find them as they rolled;
And then I knew that she was helplessly old,
As I was helplessly young.

Frances Cornford

A Birthday Poem
for Rachel

For every year of life we light
a candle on your cake
to mark the simple sort of progress
anyone can make,
and then, to test your nerve or give
a proper view of death,
you're asked to blow each light, each year,
out with your own breath.

James Simmons

This is the Day

This is the sort of day
I should like to wrap
In shiny silver paper
And only open when it's raining,

This is the sort of day
I should like to hide
In a secret drawer to which
Only I have the key,

This is the sort of day
I should like to hang
At the back of the wardrobe
To keep me warm when winter comes,

This is the day
I should like to last for ever,

This is my birthday.

June Crebbin

I am …

I am all the things of my past—
the light hair of my dad.
I am all I see and hear—
my dog jumping and licking people
and running around the yard
going crazy;
Charlie and Olga arguing all the time,
police sirens wailing in the street,
cars conking out in the middle of the street.
I am all I have been taught and I remember—
trying to speak proper Italian,
starting primary school,
and everyone crying.

Rosie Martorana

Children's Song

We live in our own world,
A world that is too small
For you to stoop and enter
Even on hands and knees,
The adult subterfuge.
And though you probe and pry
With analytic eye,
And eavesdrop all our talk
With an amused look,
You cannot find the centre
Where we dance, where we play,
Where life is still asleep
Under the closed flower,
Under the smooth shell
Of eggs in the cupped nest
That mock the faded blue
Of your remoter heaven.

R. S. Thomas

Late Home

I looked up—the sun had gone down
Though it was there a minute before
And the light had grown terribly thin
And no one played by the shore
Of the lake, now empty, and still;
And I heard the park-keepers shout
As they cycled around the paths . . .
'Closing, closing . . . everyone out . . .'

Then I panicked and started to run,
Leaving all of my friends behind
(I could hear their cries in the bushes—
It was me they were trying to find)
But they had the burn and the minnows,
The rope, the slide, the shrubbery track,
And the trees where a thrush was singing,
And I had the long road back—

The road that led, empty and straight,
Down under the tall grey flats
Where the lights were on, and the tellies,
And old ladies were putting out cats:
I ran past them, without looking round
As though I'd committed a crime:
At six they'd said 'Just half an hour'
And *now*—oh, what was the time?

How could it have gone already?
Something must be, it *must* be, wrong—
I've only just come out—and why
Does getting back take me so long?
I can't be late—or if I am,
It's the fault of the sun or the moon.
When the dentist's takes an eternity,
How are happy things over so soon?

So I stopped and asked, 'Please, mister . . .'
And his left wrist came slowly round
And he peered at his watch and shook it
And said 'Blast, it's never been wound.'
But the next man hauled his watch up,
Like a lead sinker on a line,
Clicked open the front, and boomed out,
'Right now, child, it's five to nine.'

There's a great big gap in between
The way things are, the way things seem,
And I dropped down it then, like you do
When you shoot back to life from a dream.
I stood there and muttered 'It can't be—
His watch must be wrong'—then, aghast—
'This time, I'll *really* be for it,
If it isn't a whole two hours fast.'

But I got my legs going again
And ran, gulping in red-hot air,
Through back-streets where no one knew me,
Till I came out in the Town Square.
But when I looked at the shining face
And I heard the cheerful chimes
Of the Town Hall clock—then every hope
Drained away, as it struck nine times.

Two hours late . . . two hours late—
Perhaps they've called out the police
Two hours late . . . who, all in a line,
Are combing the waste ground, piece by piece;
While *they* all stand in our window
Anxious and angry and, when I'm seen,
Ready to frown and shout 'There he is',
'Come here you!' and 'Where's the child been?'

When I come round the corner and see them,
I'll limp, as though I'd a sprain,
Then whimper 'I didn't mean it' and
'I'll never ever go out, again . . .
How can I know that time's up,
When I'm enjoying myself such a lot?
I'm sorry—won't you take me back in?
Are you glad to see me, or not?'

. . . But later in bed, as I lay there
In the extraordinary light—
Filtering through the half-drawn curtain—
Of that silvery spellbound night,
I wondered just what *had* happened
To Time, for three hours in June:
If all of my life is as happy—
Will it all be over as soon?

Brian Lee

Blackberry Picking

Late August, given heavy rain and sun
For a full week, the blackberries would ripen.
At first, just one, a glossy purple clot
Among others, red, green, hard as a knot.
You ate that first one and its flesh was sweet
Like thickened wine: summer's blood was in it
Leaving stains upon the tongue and lust for
Picking. Then red ones inked up and that hunger
Sent us out with milk-cans, pea-tins, jam-pots
Where briars scratched and wet grass bleached our boots.
Round hayfields, cornfields, and potato-drills
We trekked and picked until the cans were full,
Until the tinkling bottom had been covered
With green ones, and on top big dark blobs burned
Like a plate of eyes. Our hands were peppered
With thorn pricks, our palms sticky as Bluebeard's.

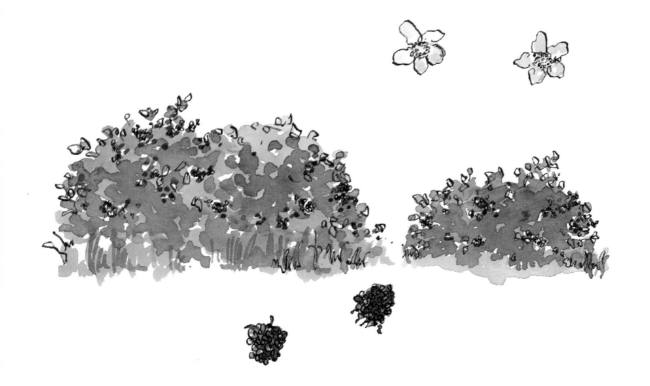

We hoarded the fresh berries in the byre.
But when the bath was filled we found a fur,
A rat-grey fungus, glutting on our cache.
The juice was stinking too. Once off the bush
The fruit fermented, the sweet flesh would turn sour.
I always felt like crying. It wasn't fair
That all the lovely canfuls smelt of rot.
Each year I hoped they'd keep, knew they would not.

Seamus Heaney

Fern Hill

Now as I was young and easy under the apple boughs
About the lilting house and happy as the grass was green,
  The night above the dingle starry,
    Time let me hail and climb
  Golden in the heydays of his eyes,
And honoured among the wagons I was prince of the apple towns
And once below a time I lordly had the trees and leaves
    Trail with daisies and barley
  Down the rivers of the windfall light.

And as I was green and carefree, famous among the barns
About the happy yard and singing as the farm was home,
  In the sun that is young once only,
    Time let me play and be
  Golden in the mercy of his means,
And green and golden I was huntsman and herdsman, the calves
Sang to my horn, the foxes on the hills barked clear and cold,
    And the sabbath rang slowly
  In the pebbles of the holy streams.

All the sun long it was running, it was lovely, the hay
Fields high as the house, the tunes from the chimneys, it was air
  And playing, lovely and watery
    And fire green as grass.
  And nightly under the simple stars
As I rode to sleep the owls were bearing the farm away,
All the moon long I heard, blessed among stables, the nightjars
  Flying with the ricks, and the horses
    Flashing into the dark.

And then to awake, and the farm, like a wanderer white
With the dew, come back, the cock on his shoulder: it was all
  Shining, it was Adam and maiden,
    The sky gathered again
  And the sun grew round that very day.
So it must have been after the birth of the simple light
In the first, spinning place, the spellbound horses walking warm
  Out of the whinnying green stable
    On to the fields of praise.

And honoured among foxes and pheasants by the gay house
Under the new made clouds and happy as the heart was long,
  In the sun born over and over,
    I ran my heedless ways,
  My wishes raced through the house high hay
And nothing I cared, at my sky blue trades, that time allows
In all his tuneful turning so few and such morning songs
  Before the children green and golden
    Follow him out of grace,

Nothing I cared, in the lamb white days, that time would take me
Up to the swallow thronged loft by the shadow of my hand,
  In the moon that is always rising,
    Nor that riding to sleep
  I should hear him fly with the high fields
And wake to the farm forever fled from the childless land.
Oh as I was young and easy in the mercy of his means,
    Time held me green and dying
  Though I sang in my chains like the sea.

Dylan Thomas

I Remember, I Remember

I remember, I remember
The house where I was born,
The little window where the sun
Came peeping in at morn;
He never came a wink too soon
Nor brought too long a day;
But now, I often wish the night
Had borne my breath away.

I remember, I remember
The roses, red and white,
The violets, and the lily-cups—
Those flowers made of light!
The lilacs where the robin built,
And where my brother set
The laburnum on his birthday,—
The tree is living yet!

I remember, I remember
Where I was used to swing,
And thought the air must rush as fresh
To swallows on the wing;
My spirit flew in feathers then
That is so heavy now,
The summer pools could hardly cool
The fever on my brow.

I remember, I remember
The fir-trees dark and high;
I used to think their slender tops
Were close against the sky:
It was a childish ignorance,
But now 'tis little joy
To know I'm farther off from Heaven
Than when I was a boy.

Thomas Hood

Names

She was Eliza for a few weeks
When she was a baby—
Eliza Lily. Soon it changed to Lil.

Later she was Miss Steward in the baker's shop
And then 'my love', 'my darling', Mother.

Widowed at thirty, she went back to work
As Mrs Hand. Her daughter grew up,
Married and gave birth.

Now she was Nanna. 'Everybody
Calls me Nanna,' she would say to visitors.
And so they did—friends, tradesmen, the doctor.

In the geriatric ward
They used the patients' Christian names.
'Lil,' we said, 'or Nanna,'
But it wasn't in her file
And for those last bewildered weeks
She was Eliza once again.

Wendy Cope

Long Sight in Age

They say eyes clear with age,
As dew clarifies air
To sharpen evenings,
As if time put an edge
Round the last shape of things
To show them there;
The many-levelled trees,
The long soft tides of grass
Wrinkling away the gold
Wind-ridden waves—all these,
They say, come back to focus
As we grow old.

Philip Larkin

Old Man Know-All

Old Man Know-All, he comes around
With his nose in the air, turned away from the ground.
His old hair hadn't been combed for weeks.
He said, 'Keep still while Know-All speaks.'

Old Man Know-All's tongue did run.
He knew everything under the sun.
When you knew one thing, he knew more.
He talked enough to make a hearing aid sore.

Old Man Know-All died last week.
He got drowned in the middle of the creek.
The bridge was there and there to stay—
But he knew too much to cross that way.

Traditional

An Old Man

Look at him there on the wet road,
Muffled with smoke, an old man trying
Time's treacherous ice with a slow foot.
Tears on his cheek are the last glitter
On bare branches of the long storm
That shook him once leaving him bowed
And destitute as a tree stripped
Of foliage under a bald sky.

Come, then, winter, build with your cold
Hands a bridge over those depths
His mind balks at; let him go on,
Confident still; let the hard hammer
Of pain fall with as light a blow
On the brow's anvil as the sun does now.

R. S. Thomas

The Old Men Admiring Themselves in the Water

I heard the old, old men say,
'Everything alters,
And one by one we drop away.'
They had hands like claws, and their knees
Were twisted like the old thorn-trees
By the waters.
I heard the old men say,
'All that's beautiful drifts away
Like the waters.'

W. B. Yeats

'Body Grows Old, Heart Stays Young'

Before we troubled
The Cape of Storms
Or shook the Highveld
With horses and arms,
Before the births
Of Shaka, Retief,
Old Zulus were chanting
This joy-in-grief:
'Body grows old,
Heart stays young.'
Such was the heartsease
In their song.

Now, as we drive
Or are driven apart
Till none dare give
Of the love in his heart,
As bodies grow chill
As spears to each other
And clouds drift still
Through ominous weather,
'Hearts grow old
In bodies yet young,'
Runs like a shudder
Through our song.

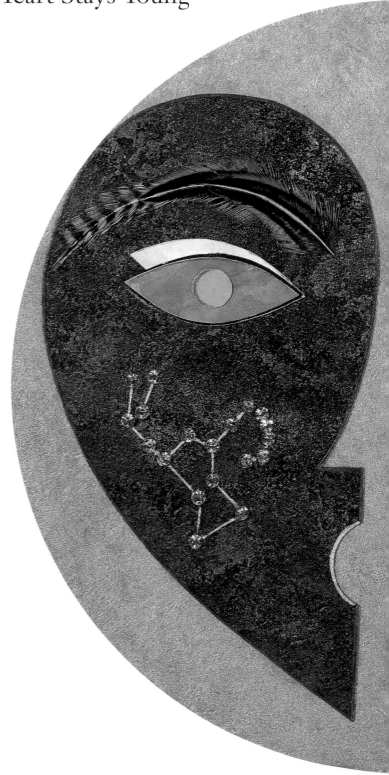

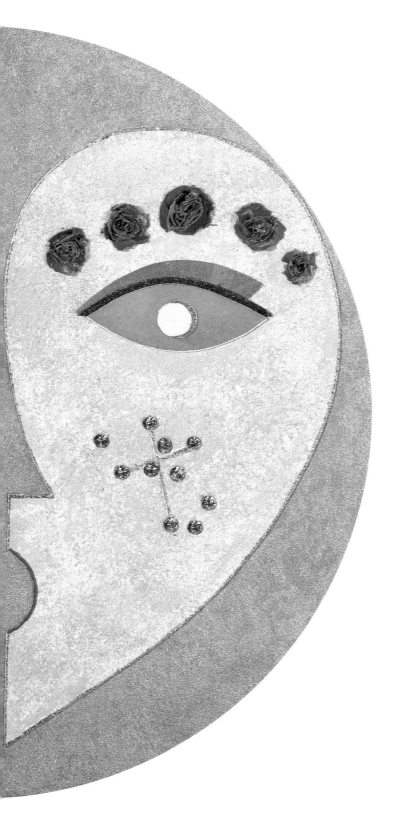

In ages of iron
Gilded with gold
The Cross and Orion
Swing high and cold.
Great Hunter, Great Lover,
Swing low, shine warm
Till our tongues recover
That ancient charm:
'Body grows old,
Heart stays young'
Again be the sequence
Of all song.

Guy Butler

Warning

When I am an old woman I shall wear purple
With a red hat which doesn't go, and doesn't suit me.
And I shall spend my pension on brandy and summer gloves
And satin sandals, and say we've no money for butter.
I shall sit down on the pavement when I'm tired
And gobble up samples in shops and press alarm bells
And run my stick along the public railings
And make up for the sobriety of my youth.
I shall go out in my slippers in the rain
And pick the flowers in other people's gardens
And learn to spit.

You can wear terrible shirts and grow more fat
And eat three pounds of sausages at a go
Or only bread and pickle for a week
And hoard pens and pencils and beermats and things in boxes.

But now we must have clothes that keep us dry
And pay our rent and not swear in the street
And set a good example for the children.
We must have friends to dinner and read the papers.

But maybe I ought to practise a little now?
So people who know me are not too shocked and surprised
When suddenly I am old, and start to wear purple.

Jenny Joseph

130

A Long Time Ago

A long time ago
there was a man who lived round our way
and he said:
'When I die,
I don't want to be buried in the ground
I want to be buried in the air.'
So he set about making sure
he would be buried in the air.
He got people to build him a big yellow tower.
He said, 'I want to be buried half-way up this tower.'
Not long after, he died.
When they came to bury him
they decided that they didn't want to bury him
in the air, half-way up the tower,
so they buried him in the ground instead
and there was nothing on earth he could do about it.
But the tower's still there
and everyone knows it was built for the man
who wanted to be buried in the air
but couldn't make sure he would be.

Michael Rosen

Looking Forward

The days are getting longer.
From my first-floor window
I can sit and watch
the tide of people ebb and flow.
I know them all
the early-morning milkman
postman
paperboy
the schoolchild
worker
shopper.
I invent their lives.
Now I have started looking forward
to the sights and sounds
of summer evenings
by my open window
children playing late
lawnmowers
couples walking dogs.
And yet
perhaps this summer I shall not be here.
My days are getting shorter.

Sue Cowling

Into My Heart

Into my heart an air that kills
  From yon far country blows:
What are those blue remembered hills,
  What spires, what farms are those?

That is the land of lost content,
  I see it shining plain,
The happy highways where I went
  And cannot come again.

A. E. Housman

Song

When I am dead, my dearest,
  Sing no sad songs for me;
Plant thou no roses at my head,
  Nor shady cypress tree:
Be the green grass above me
  With showers and dewdrops wet;
And if thou wilt, remember,
  And if thou wilt, forget.

I shall not see the shadows,
  I shall not feel the rain;
I shall not hear the nightingale
  Sing on, as if in pain:
And dreaming through the twilight
  That doth not rise nor set,
Haply I may remember,
  And haply may forget.

Christina Rossetti

The Fly

Little Fly,
Thy summer's play
My thoughtless hand
Has brush'd away.

Am not I
A fly like thee?
Or art not thou
A man like me?

For I dance,
And drink, and sing,
Till some blind hand
Shall brush my wing.

William Blake

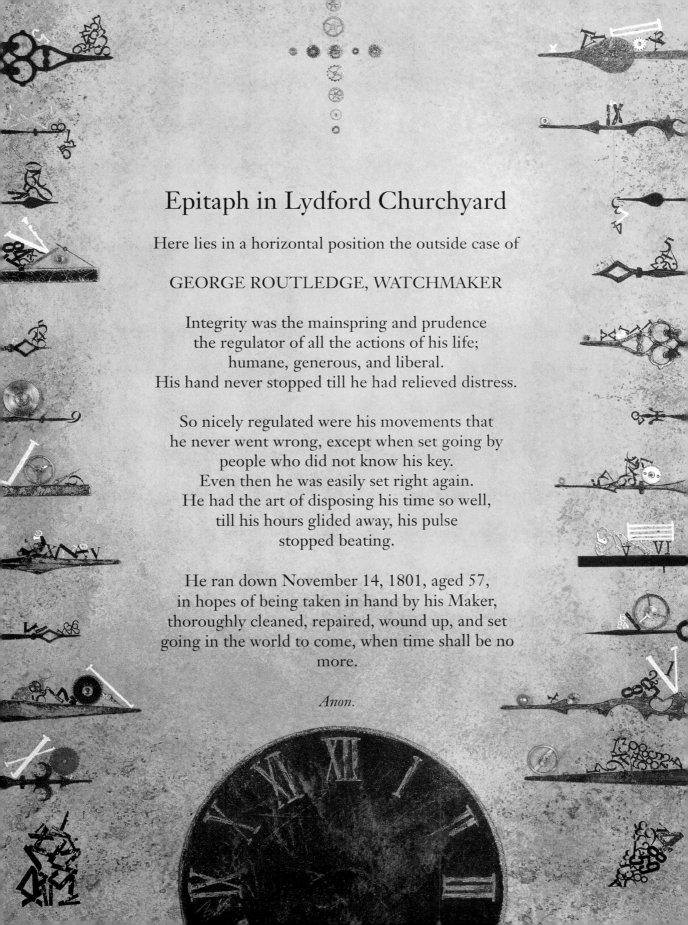

Epitaph in Lydford Churchyard

Here lies in a horizontal position the outside case of

GEORGE ROUTLEDGE, WATCHMAKER

Integrity was the mainspring and prudence
the regulator of all the actions of his life;
humane, generous, and liberal.
His hand never stopped till he had relieved distress.

So nicely regulated were his movements that
he never went wrong, except when set going by
people who did not know his key.
Even then he was easily set right again.
He had the art of disposing his time so well,
till his hours glided away, his pulse
stopped beating.

He ran down November 14, 1801, aged 57,
in hopes of being taken in hand by his Maker,
thoroughly cleaned, repaired, wound up, and set
going in the world to come, when time shall be no
more.

Anon.

Lines said to have been Written on the Eve of his Execution

Even such is Time, which takes in trust
  Our youth, our joys, and all we have,
And pays us but with age and dust,
  Which in the dark and silent grave,
When we have wandered all our ways,
Shuts up the story of our days;
  But from this earth, this grave, this dust,
  My God shall raise me up, I trust.

Sir Walter Raleigh

In a Disused Graveyard

The living come with grassy tread
To read the gravestones on the hill;
The graveyard draws the living still,
But never anymore the dead.

The verses in it say and say:
'The ones who living come today
To read the stones and go away
Tomorrow dead will come to stay.'

So sure of death the marbles rhyme,
Yet can't help marking all the time
How no one dead will seem to come.
What is it men are shrinking from?

It would be easy to be clever
And tell the stones: Men hate to die
And have stopped dying now forever.
I think they would believe the lie.

Robert Frost

Uphill

Does the road wind uphill all the way?
　　Yes, to the very end.
Will the day's journey take the whole long day?
　　From morn to night, my friend.

But is there for the night a resting-place?
　　A roof for when the slow, dark hours begin.
May not the darkness hide it from my face?
　　You cannot miss that inn.

Shall I meet other wayfarers at night?
　　Those who have gone before.
Then must I knock, or call when just in sight?
　　They will not keep you waiting at that door.

Shall I find comfort, travel-sore and weak?
　　Of labour you shall find the sum.
Will there be beds for me and all who seek?
　　Yea, beds for all who come.

Christina Rossetti

Fear No More the Heat o' the Sun

Fear no more the heat o' the sun,
Nor the furious winter's rages;
Thou thy worldly task hast done,
Home art gone, and ta'en thy wages.
Golden lads and girls all must,
As chimney-sweepers, come to dust.

Fear no more the frown o' the great,
Thou art past the tyrant's stroke;
Care no more to clothe and eat,
To thee the reed is as the oak.
The sceptre, learning, physic, must,
All follow this, and come to dust.

Fear no more the lightning-flash,
Nor the all-dreaded thunder-stone;
Fear not slander, censure rash;
Thou hast finished joy and moan.
All lovers young, all lovers must
Consign to thee, and come to dust.

No exorcisor harm thee,
Nor no witchcraft charm thee.
Ghost unlaid forbear thee.
Nothing ill come near thee.
Quiet consummation have,
And renownèd be thy grave.

William Shakespeare

Do Not Go Gentle into that Good Night

Do not go gentle into that good night.
Old age should burn and rave at close of day;
Rage, rage against the dying of the light.

Though wise men at their end know dark is right,
Because their words had forked no lightning they
Do not go gentle into that good night.

Good men, the last wave by, crying how bright
Their frail deeds might have danced in a green bay,
Rage, rage against the dying of the light.

Wild men who caught and sang the sun in flight,
And learn, too late, they grieved it on its way,
Do not go gentle into that good night.

Grave men, near death, who see with blinding sight
Blind eyes could blaze like meteors and be gay,
Rage, rage against the dying of the light.

And you, my father, there on the sad height,
Curse, bless, me now with your fierce tears, I pray.
Do not go gentle into that good night.
Rage, rage against the dying of the light.

Dylan Thomas

Prospero's Farewell to his Magic

Our revels now are ended. These our actors,
As I foretold you, were all spirits and
Are melted into air, into thin air:
And, like the baseless fabric of this vision,
The cloud-capp'd towers, the gorgeous palaces,
The solemn temples, the great globe itself,
Yea, all which it inherit, shall dissolve
And, like this insubstantial pageant faded,
Leave not a rack behind. We are such stuff
As dreams are made on, and our little life
Is rounded with a sleep.

William Shakespeare

Fire and Ice

Some say the world will end in fire,
Some say in ice.
From what I've tasted of desire
I hold with those who favour fire.
But if it had to perish twice,
I think I know enough of hate
To say that for destruction ice
Is also great
And would suffice.

Robert Frost

The Judgement Flood

The great storm will come when Monday's a day,
 All the world of the air will outpour,
And through all its lasting we shall obey,
 We whose ears will be filled with its roar.

The freezing will come when Tuesday's a day,
 All pain to the heart and piercing fine,
Flecking from the cheeks, though pale of array,
 Blood as red as the red-pouring wine.

The wind it will blow when Wednesday's a day,
 Sweeping bare down the strath and the plain,
Sharp-showering the gusts that cut and slay,
 Thunderclaps and mountains split in twain.

The rain it will pour when Thursday's a day,
 Driving men into blind rushing flight,
Faster than leaves which scurry from the spray,
 A-shake like Mary's plant-leaves in fright.

The dark cloud will come when Friday's a day,
 The direst dread that ever was known,
Multitudes left with their reason astray,
 Grass and fish underneath the one stone.

The great sea will come when Saturday's a day,
 Full of anger, full of sorrow's pain,
As he hears the bitter words all men say,
 A red cross on each right shoulder lain.

Anon.

The Four Horsemen

And I saw when the Lamb opened one of the seals,
and I heard, as it were the noise of thunder,
one of the four beasts saying, Come and see.
And I saw, and behold a white horse:
and he that sat on him had a bow;
and a crown was given unto him:
and he went forth conquering, and to conquer.

And when he had opened the second seal,
I heard the second beast say, Come and see.
And there went out another horse that was red:
and power was given to him that sat thereon
to take peace from the earth,
and that they should kill one another:
and there was given unto him a great sword.

And when he had opened the third seal,
I heard the third beast say, Come and see.
And I beheld, and lo a black horse;
and he that sat on him had a pair of balances in his hand.
And I heard a voice in the midst of the four beasts say,
A measure of wheat for a penny,
and three measures of barley for a penny;
and see thou hurt not the oil and the wine.

And when he had opened the fourth seal,
I heard the voice of the fourth beast say, Come and see.
And I looked and behold a pale horse:
and his name that sat on him was Death,
and Hell followed with him.
And power was given unto them over the fourth part of the earth,
to kill with a sword,
and with hunger,
and with death,
and with the beasts of the earth.

Revelation 6: 1–8
The Bible: King James Version

The Last Days

But in the last days it shall come to pass,
that the mountain of the house of the Lord
shall be established in the top of the mountains,
and it shall be exalted above the hills;
and people shall flow unto it.
And many nations shall come, and say,
Come, and let us go up to the mountain of the Lord,
and to the house of the God of Jacob;
and he will teach us of his ways,
and we will walk in his paths:
for the law shall go forth of Zion,
and the word of the Lord from Jerusalem.

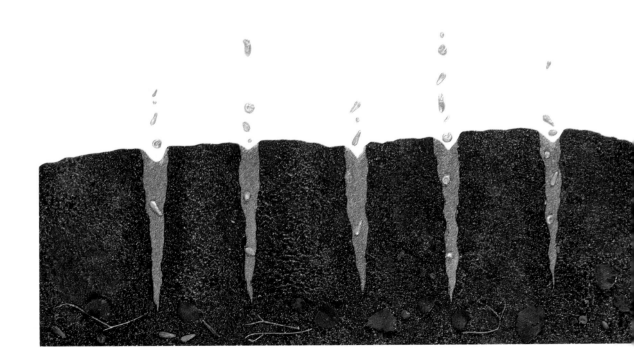

And he shall judge among many people,
and rebuke strong nations afar off;
and they shall beat their swords into plowshares,
and their spears into pruninghooks:
nation shall not lift up a sword against nation,
neither shall they learn war any more.
But they shall sit every man under his vine
and under his fig tree;
and none shall make them afraid:
for the mouth of the Lord of Hosts hath spoken it.

Micah 4: 1–4
The Bible: King James Version

And Death Shall Have no Dominion

And death shall have no dominion.
Dead men naked they shall be one
With the man in the wind and the west moon;
When their bones are picked clean and the clean bones gone,
They shall have stars at elbow and foot;
Though they go mad they shall be sane,
Though they sink through the sea they shall rise again;
Though lovers be lost love shall not;
And death shall have no dominion.

And death shall have no dominion.
Under the windings of the sea
They lying long shall not die windily;
Twisting on racks when sinews give way,
Strapped to a wheel, yet they shall not break;
Faith in their hands shall snap in two,
And the unicorn evils run them through;
Split all ends up they shan't crack;
And death shall have no dominion.

And death shall have no dominion.
No more may gulls cry at their ears
Or waves break loud on the seashores;
Where blew a flower may a flower no more
Lift its head to the blows of the rain;
Though they be mad and dead as nails,
Heads of the characters hammer through daisies;
Break in the sun till the sun breaks down,
And death shall have no dominion.

Dylan Thomas

Index of Titles and First Lines

(*First lines are in italic*)

A breeze wipes creases off my forehead 48
A long time ago 130
A poem is 157
A potato clock, a potato clock 18
'About 7000 years ago 102
Adlestrop 49
All Hushed and Still 78
All hushed and still within the house 78
And Death Shall Have no Dominion 150
And God stepped out on space 32
And I saw when the Lamb opened one of the seals 147
And when our streets are green again 85
Answer July 75
April Rise 22
As I Walked out one Evening 66
from Auguries of Innocence 99

BC:AD 45
Before we troubled 126
Big clocks go tick 19
Birthday Poem, A 106
Blackberry Picking 114
'Body Grows Old, Heart Stays Young' 126
Broad sun-stoned beaches 41
Burnt Norton 61
But in the last days it shall come to pass 148

Child at the Window, The 104
Childhood 105
Children's Song 109
Come back from summer 50
Comparison, A 63
Composed upon Westminster Bridge 40
Creation, The 32

Day came in 39
Day in Autumn, A 44
Days 89
Do Not Go Gentle into that Good Night 140
Does the road wind uphill all the way? 138
Doing My Homework 25
Doing my homework last night 25
Dover Beach 70

Earth has not anything to show more fair 40
Egypt's Might is Tumbled Down 81
Epitaph in Lydford Churchyard 135
Even such is Time, which takes in trust 136
Every night and every morn 99

Fear No More the Heat o' the Sun 139
Fern Hill 116
Fire and Ice 143
Fly, The 134
For every year of life we light 106
Four Horsemen, The 147

Gather ye rosebuds while ye may 93

Had we but world enough, and time 94
Half-Past Two 14
Here lies in a horizontal position the outside case of 135
How long ago Hector took off his plume 80
How many seconds in a minute? 4
How Many? 4
Humming-Bird 38

I am all the things of my past 108
I am . . . 108
I can imagine, in some otherworld 38
I found this jawbone at the sea's edge 83
I heard the old, old men say 125
I looked up—the sun had gone down 110
I met a traveller from an antique land 82
I Remember, I Remember 119
I Stood on a Tower in the Wet 46
i thank You God 31
i thank You God for most this amazing 31
I used to think that grown-up people chose 105
I went to school a day too soon 43
I'll tell you, shall I, something I remember? 56
I've known rivers 64
If ever I saw blessing in the air 22
If I Could Tell You 74
In a dark stone 102
In a Disused Graveyard 137
In Snapshotland everyone is happy all the time 52
Infant Sorrow 97
Into My Heart 132
Into my heart an air that kills 132
Is that child in the snapshot me? 54
It was Long Ago 56
It was the time of year 47
It will not always be like this 44

Jenny kissed me when we met 59
Judgement Flood, The 144

Last Days, The 148

Late August, given heavy rain and sun   114
Late Home   110
Leisure   92
Like as the Waves   72
Like as the waves make towards the pebbled shore   72
Lines said to have been Written on the Eve of his Execution   136
Little Fly / Thy summer's play   134
Lock up Your Clocks   16
Long Sight in Age   122
Long Time Ago, A   130
Look at him there on the wet road   124
Looking Forward   131
Love set you going like a fat gold watch   98
Loveliest of Trees   23
Loveliest of trees, the cherry now   23

Midsummer, Tobago   41
Morning   39
Morning Song   98
My mother groan'd, my father wept   97

Names   121
Negro Speaks of Rivers, The   64
Night will Never Stay, The   79
Nothing is so beautiful as Spring   84
Now as I was young and easy under the apple boughs   116
Nurse's Song   100
Nurse's Song   101

Off to Outer Space Tomorrow Morning   30
Old Man, An   124
Old Man Know-All   123
Old Man Know-All, he comes around   123
Old Men Admiring Themselves in the Water, The   125
On Finding an Old Photograph   51
On his Blindness   96
On the Vanity of Earthly Greatness   88
Once that Never Was, The   27
Once upon a schooltime   14
Ostrich is a Silly Bird, The   26
Our revels now are ended. These our actors   142
Ozymandias   82

Parting in Wartime   80
Piano   58
Poem in June   48
Poem Is, A   157
Potato Clock   18
Prehistoric Camp, A   47
Prospero's Farewell to his Magic   142

Quieter than Snow   43

Relic   83
Remember this, when childhood's far away   104
Road not Taken, The   60
Rondeau   59

September   50
She was Eliza for a few weeks   121
Small Dawn Song   21
Snapshotland   52
Softly, in the dusk, a woman is singing to me   58
Some say the world will end in fire   143
Song (McGrath)   85
Song (Rossetti)   133
Spell of Creation   36
Spring   84
Strap me in your time machine   28
Sunset   42

Talking Time-Travel Blues   28
The days are getting longer   131
The grandfather clock in the hall   16
The great storm will come when Monday's a day   144
The lapse of time and rivers is the same   63
The living come with grassy tread   137
The night will never stay   79
The Once that Never Was may be   27
The ostrich is a silly bird   26
The sea is calm tonight   70
the sun / is having its last fling   42
The tusks that clashed in mighty brawls   88
They say eyes clear with age   122
They shut the road through the woods   86
This is just to say Thank You   21
This is the Day   107
This is the sort of day   107
This was the moment when Before   45
Three or So   54
Tick-Tock Talk   19
Time present and time past   61
Time will say nothing but I told you so   74
To Everything There Is a Season   90
To His Coy Mistress   94
To the Virgins, to Make Much of Time   93
Tomorrow Wonders   24
Two roads diverged in a yellow wood   60

Uncle Time   77
Uncle Time is a ole, ole man . . .   77
Uphill   138

Warning   128
Way through the Woods, The   86
We live in our own world   109
What are days for?   89
What is this life if, full of care   92

'What will they bring me, I wonder?' 24
When I am an old woman I shall wear purple
  128
When I am dead, my dearest 133
When I consider how my light is spent 96
When the voices of children are heard on the green
  100
When the voices of children are heard on the green
  101

Who is that child I see wandering, wandering 73
Who? 73
Will There Really Be a 'Morning'? 13
Within the flower there lies a seed 36

Yalding, 1912. My father 51
Yes. I remember Adlestrop 49
You can start the Count Down, you can take a last
  look 30

Index of Authors

Acorn, Milton 48
Anon. 135, 144
Arnold, Matthew 70
Auden, W. H. 66, 74

Blake, William 97, 99, 100, 101, 134
Brand, Dionne 39
Brontë, Emily 78
Butler, Guy 126

Causley, Charles 73
Coleridge, Mary 81
Cope, Wendy 51, 121
Corben, John 25
Cornford, Frances 80, 105
Cowling, Sue 131
Cowper, William 63
Crebbin, June 42, 107
Cummings, E. E. 31

Davies, W. H. 92
Dickinson, Emily 13, 75
Doherty, Berlie 43, 54

Ecclesiastes 90
Eliot, T. S. 61

Fanthorpe, U. A. 14, 15
Farjeon, Eleanor 56, 79
Freeman, Mary E. Wilkins 26
Frost, Robert 60, 137, 143

Giles, Barbara 27
Gross, Philip 16, 21
Guiterman, Arthur 88

Heaney, Seamus 114
Herrick, Robert 93
Hoban, Russell 24
Hood, Thomas 119
Hopkins, Gerard Manley 84
Housman, A. E. 23, 132
Hughes, Langston 64
Hughes, Ted 83
Hunt, James Leigh 59

Johnson, James Weldon 32
Joseph, Jenny 102, 128

Kantaris, Sylvia 52
Kipling, Rudyard 86

Larkin, Philip 89, 122
Lawrence, D. H. 38, 58
Lee, Brian 110
Lee, Laurie 22

Martorana, Rosie 108
Marvell, Andrew 94
McCord, David 19
McGough, Roger 18
McGrath, John 85
Micah 148
Milton, John 96
Mole, John 50

Nicholson, Norman 30

Plath, Sylvia 98

Raine, Kathleen 36
Raleigh, Sir Walter 136
Revelation 146
Rosen, Michael 130
Rossetti, Christina 4, 133, 138
Rumble, Adrian 28

Sassoon, Siegfried 104
Scott, Dennis 77
Shakespeare, William 72, 139, 142
Shelley, Percy Bysshe 82
Simmons, James 106
Stallworthy, Jon 157

Tennyson, Alfred, Lord 46
Thomas, Dylan 116, 140, 150
Thomas, Edward 49
Thomas, R. S. 44, 109, 124
Traditional 123

Walcott, Derek 41
Wordsworth, William 40

Yeats, W. B. 125
Young, Andrew 47

Index of Artists

Elaine Cox   pp. 36/37, 49, 70/71, 83, 102/103, 126/127,135,148/149;

Madeleine Floyd   pp. 26, 56/57, 84/85, 92/93, 96, 114/115, 124/125;

Clare Hemstock   pp. 13, 31, 51, 63, 73, 89, 97, 121, 133, 143;

Sharon Lewis   pp. 16/17, 54, 86/87, 106/107, 110/111/112/113, 130/131;

Charlie Mackesey   pp. 12, 22/23, 32/33/34/35,78/79, 99, 119, 132;

Alan Marks   pp. 20/21, 40/41, 52/53, 66/67/68/69, 80/81, 104/105, 140/141, 150/151;

Debra McFarlane   pp. 24/25, 60, 76/77, 94/95, 116/117/118, 128/129, 136, 142;

Mary McQuillan   pp. 18/19, 28/29, 42, 88, 122/123;

Sara van Niekerk   pp. 38, 45, 91, 138/139, 146;

Rachel Pearce   pp. 15, 46/47, 64/65, 100/101, 108/109, 144/145

Acknowledgements

The editors and publisher are grateful for permission to include the following copyright material:

Extracts from the *Authorized Version of the Bible (The King James Bible)*, the rights in which are vested in the Crown, are reproduced by permission of the Crown's Patentee, Cambridge University Press. **Milton Acorn:** 'Poem in June' reprinted from *Dig Up My Heart* by Milton Acorn, by permission of McClelland & Stewart, Inc., The Canadian Publishers. **W.H. Auden:** 'As I Walked Out One Evening' and 'If I Could Tell You' both reprinted from *Collected Poems* edited by Edward Mendelson, Copyright 1940 by W.H. Auden, Copyright © 1976 by Edward Mendelson, William Meredith, and Monroe K. Spears, Executors of the Estate of W.H. Auden, by permission of the publishers, Faber & Faber Ltd and Random House Inc. **Guy Butler:** 'Body Grows Old, Heart Stays Young' reprinted from *Songs and Ballads* (David Philip, 1978), by permission of Professor G. Butler. **Charles Causley:** 'Who?' reprinted from *Figgie Hobbin* (Macmillan), by permission of David Higham Associates. **John Corben:** 'Doing My Homework' reprinted from *Junk Mail* by Michael Harrison (OUP, 1993), by permission of the author. **Wendy Cope:** 'On Finding an Old Photograph' reprinted from *Making Cocoa for Kingsley Amis*, by permission of the publishers, Faber & Faber Ltd; and 'Names' reprinted from *Serious Concerns*, by permission of the publishers, Faber & Faber Ltd. **Frances Cornford:** 'Parting in Wartime' and 'Childhood' both reprinted from *Collected Poems* (Cresset Press), by permission of Hutchinson, Random House UK Ltd. **Sue Cowling:** 'Looking Forward' reprinted from *What is a Kumquat*, by permission of the publishers, Faber & Faber Ltd. **June Crebbin:** 'Sunset' and 'This is the Day' both reprinted from *The Dinosaur's Dinner* (Viking, 1992), Copyright © June Crebbin 1992, by permission of Penguin Books Ltd. **E.E. Cummings:** 'i thank you god for most this amazing' reprinted from *Complete Poems 1904–1962* by E.E. Cummings, edited by George J. Firmage, Copyright © 1991 by the Trustees for the E.E. Cummings Trust and George J. Firmage, by permission of W.W. Norton & Company Ltd. **W.H. Davies:** 'Leisure' reprinted from *Complete Poems* (Jonathan Cape), by permission of Random House UK Ltd on behalf of the Executors of the W.H. Davies Estate. **Emily Dickinson:** poem # 101 ('Will There Really Be a "Morning"') and poem # 386 ('Answer July'), reprinted from *The Poems of Emily Dickinson* edited by Thomas H. Johnson (The Belknap Press of Harvard University Press, Cambridge, Mass.), Copyright © 1951, 1955, 1979, 1983 by the President and Fellows of Harvard College, by permission of the publishers and the Trustees of Amherst College; poem # 386 also reprinted from *The Complete Poems of Emily Dickinson* edited by Thomas H. Johnson (Little, Brown and Company, Boston), Copyright 1929, 1935 by Martha Dickinson Bianchi, Copyright © renewed 1957, 1963 by Mary L. Hampson, by permission of Little, Brown and Company. **Berlie Doherty:** 'Three or So' and 'Quieter than Snow' both reprinted from *Walking on Air* (Lions), by permission of David Higham Associates. **T.S. Eliot:** lines from 'Burnt Norton' in *Four Quartets*, Copyright 1943 by T.S. Eliot and renewed 1971 by Esme Valerie Eliot, reprinted from *Collected Poems 1909–1962*, by permission of the publishers, Faber & Faber Ltd and Harcourt Brace & Company. **U.A. Fanthorpe:** 'Half-Past Two', Copyright U.A. Fanthorpe, reprinted from *Neck Verse* (1992); and 'BC:AD', Copyright U.A. Fanthorpe, reprinted from *Poems for Christmas* (1981) both by permission of Peterloo Poets. **Eleanor Farjeon:** 'It was Long Ago' and 'The Night Will Never Stay' both reprinted from *Silver-Sand and Snow* (Michael Joseph), by permission of David Higham Associates. **Robert Frost:** 'The Road Not Taken', 'Fire and Ice', and 'In A Disused Graveyard' all reprinted from *The Poetry of Robert Frost* edited by Edward Connery Lathem (Jonathan Cape/Henry Holt), Copyright 1942, 1944, 1951, © 1962 by Robert Frost, © 1970 by Lesley Frost Ballantine, Copyright 1916, 1923, 1934, © 1969 by Henry Holt and Company, Inc., by permission of Henry Holt and Company, Inc. and Random House UK Ltd on behalf of the Estate of Robert Frost. **Barbara Giles:** 'The Once that Never Was' reprinted from *Upright Downfall* (OUP), by permission of the author. **Philip Gross:** 'Lock up Your Clocks' and 'Small Dawn Song' both reprinted from *All-Nite Café*, by permission of the publishers, Faber & Faber Ltd. **Arthur Guiterman:** 'On the Vanity of Earthly Greatness' reprinted from *Poem for the Day*

A Poem Is

A poem is
something that someone is saying
no louder, Pip, than my 'goodnight'—
words with a tune, which outstaying
their speaker travel as far
as that amazing, vibrant light
from a long-extinguished star.

Jon Stallworthy

Ah, fill the Cup:— what boots it to repeat
How Time is slipping underneath our Feet

Take things as they come
All things pass

Time is but the stream I go a-fishing in

What seest thou else
In the dark backward and abysm of time